M000036251

Financial & Managerial Accounting or Corporate Financial Accounting

FOURTEENTH EDITION

Carl S. Warren
Professor Emeritus of Accounting
University of Georgia, Athens

James M. Reeve
Professor Emeritus of Accounting
University of Tennessee, Knoxville

Jonathan E. Duchac
Professor of Accounting
Wake Forest University

CENGAGE

Australia • Brazil • Mexico • Singapore • United Kingdom • United States

CENGAGE

For product information and technology assistance, contact us at
**Cengage Academic Resource Center,
1-800-423-0563**.

For permission to use material from this text or product, submit all requests online at **www.cengage.com/permissions**. Further permissions questions can be emailed to **permissionrequest@cengage.com**.

ISBN: 978-1-305-87883-9

Cengage
20 Channel Center Street
Boston, MA 02210
USA

Cengage is a leading provider of customized learning solutions with employees residing in nearly 40 different countries and sales in more than 125 countries around the world. Find your local representative at **www.cengage.com**.

Cengage products are represented in Canada by Nelson Education, Ltd.

To learn more about Cengage platforms and services, register or access your online learning solution, or purchase materials for your course, visit **www.cengage.com**.

Printed in the United States of America
2 3 4 5 6   22 21 20 19 18

CONTENTS

(The online appendix Working Papers are available at www.cengagebrain.com.)

The working papers include problem-specific forms for preparing solutions for Exercises, A&B Problems, the Continuing Problem, and the Comprehensive Problems from the textbook. These forms, with preprinted headings, provide a structure for the problems, which will help you get started and save you time.

Based on students' testimonials and instructors' feedback, the forms in the working papers have been streamlined to make them simpler to use and to better reflect the changing environment of business. For example, the vertical rules that separated digits of numbers entered into journals, ledgers, and statements have been removed, making it easier to write in numbers.

Note that when entering whole amounts into the forms, your instructor will direct you on whether to include a decimal point and zeroes (e.g., 100.00) or to omit those (e.g., 100).

EXERCISE 1-1

A. 1. _____   6. _____   11. _____

2. _____   7. _____   12. _____

3. _____   8. _____   13. _____

4. _____   9. _____   14. _____

5. _____   10. _____   15. _____

B. _____

_____

_____

EXERCISE 1-2

_____

_____

_____

_____

_____

_____

_____

_____

_____

EXERCISE 1-3

A. 1. _____   6. _____

2. _____   7. _____

3. _____   8. _____

4. _____   9. _____

5. _____   10. _____

B. _____

_____

_____

EXERCISE 1-4

_____

_____

EXERCISE 1-5

_____

_____

EXERCISE 1-6

	Assets	=	Liabilities	+	Stockholders' Equity
A.	_____	=	$550,000	+	$1,345,000
B.	$776,500	=	_____	+	$588,800
C.	$14,750,000	=	$4,455,000	+	_____

EXERCISE 1-7

A. _____

B. _____

C. _____

D. _____

E. _____

EXERCISE 1-8

A. _____

B. _____

C. _____

D. _____

E. _____

F. _____

EXERCISE 1-9

A. _____

B. _____

C. _____

D. _____

E. _____

EXERCISE 1-10

A. **(1)** Assets: _____

   (2) Liabilities: _____

   (3) Stockholders' equity: _____

B. **(1)** Assets: _____

   (2) Liabilities: _____

   (3) Stockholders' equity: _____

EXERCISE 1-10, Concluded

C. _____

_____

_____

_____

_____

EXERCISE 1-11

1. Expenses: _____

2. Issuing common stock in exchange for cash: _____

3. Dividends: _____

4. Revenues: _____

EXERCISE 1-12

1. _____   6. _____

2. _____   7. _____

3. _____   8. _____

4. _____   9. _____

5. _____   10. _____

EXERCISE 1-13

A. (1) _____

(2) _____

(3) _____

(4) _____

(5) _____

(6) _____

(7) _____

B. _____

C. _____

D. _____

E. _____

EXERCISE 1-14

_____

_____

_____

_____

EXERCISE 1-15

Amber:		
Blue:		
Coral:		
Daffodil:		

EXERCISE 1-16

1. Accounts Receivable: _____

2. Cash: _____

3. Common Stock: _____

4. Fees Earned: _____

5. Land: _____

6. Supplies: _____

7. Supplies Expense: _____

8. Utilities Expense: _____

9. Wages Expense: _____

10. Wages Payable: _____

EXERCISE 1-17

1. Accounts Receivable: _____

2. Cash: _____

3. Common Stock: _____

4. Fees Earned: _____

5. Land: _____

6. Supplies: _____

7. Supplies Expense: _____

8. Utilities Expense: _____

9. Wages Expense: _____

10. Wages Payable: _____

EXERCISE 1-18

A.

Retained Earnings Statement		

EXERCISE 1-18, Concluded

B. _____

_____

_____

_____

EXERCISE 1-19

Income Statement

EXERCISE 1-20

Freeman:

Heyward:

Jones:

Ramirez:

EXERCISE 1-21

A.

Balance Sheet

Balance Sheet

EXERCISE 1-21, Concluded

B.

C.

EXERCISE 1-22

A. 1. Accounts payable: _____

2. Cash equivalents: _____

3. Crude oil inventory: _____

4. Equipment: _____

5. Exploration expenses: _____

6. Income taxes payable: _____

7. Investments: _____

8. Long-term debt: _____

9. Marketable securities: _____

10. Notes and loans payable: _____

11. Notes receivable: _____

12. Operating expenses: _____

13. Prepaid taxes: _____

14. Sales: _____

15. Selling expenses: _____

B. _____

_____

_____

_____

_____

_____

EXERCISE 1-22, Concluded

C. _____

_____

_____

EXERCISE 1-23

1. Cash received from fees earned: _____

2. Cash paid for expenses: _____

3. Cash paid for land: _____

4. Cash paid to owner for dividends: _____

EXERCISE 1-24

Statement of Cash Flows		

EXERCISE 1-25

_____

_____

_____

_____

_____

_____

_____

_____

_____

_____

_____

_____

_____

_____

_____

_____

_____

_____

_____

_____

_____

_____

_____

_____

_____

_____

_____

_____

_____

_____

_____

_____

_____

EXERCISE 1-25, Continued

(Optional)

Income Statement

Retained Earnings Statement

EXERCISE 1-25, Concluded

(Optional)

Balance Sheet			

This Page Not Used.

PROBLEM 1-1 _____

1.

	ASSETS			=	LIABILITIES	+				STOCKHOLDERS' EQUITY				
	Cash	+	Accounts Receivable	+	Supplies	=	Accounts Payable	+	Common Stock	−	Dividends	+	Fees Earned	−	Rent Expense	−	Salaries Expense	−	Supplies Expense	−	Auto Expense	−	Misc. Expense

A. _____

B. _____

Bal. _____

C. _____

Bal. _____

D. _____

Bal. _____

E. _____

Bal. _____

F. _____

Bal. _____

G. _____

Bal. _____

H. _____

Bal. _____

I. _____

Bal. _____

J. _____

Bal. _____

PROBLEM 1-1 ___, Concluded

2. _____
_____
_____
_____

3. _____
_____

4. _____
_____
_____
_____

PROBLEM 1-2 ___

1.

	Income Statement		

2.

	Retained Earnings Statement		

PROBLEM 1-2 ___, Concluded

3.

Balance Sheet		

4. _____

_____

_____

_____

_____

_____

PROBLEM 1-3 ___

1.

	Income Statement		

2.

	Retained Earnings Statement		

PROBLEM 1-3 ___, Continued

3.

Balance Sheet		

PROBLEM 1-3 ___ , Concluded

4. (Optional)

Statement of Cash Flows		

This Page Not Used.

PROBLEM 1-4 _____

1.

	ASSETS		=	LIABILITIES	+		STOCKHOLDERS' EQUITY						
	Cash	+ Supplies	=	Accounts Payable	+ Common Stock	− Dividends	+ Sales Comm.	− Rent Expense	− Salaries Expense	− Auto Expense	− Supplies Expense	− Misc. Expense
A.												
B.												
Bal.												
C.												
Bal.												
D.												
Bal.												
E.												
Bal.												
F.												
Bal.												
G.												
Bal.												
H.												
Bal.												
I.												
Bal.												

PROBLEM 1-4 ___, Continued

2.

	Income Statement		

	Retained Earnings Statement		

PROBLEM 1-4 ___ , Concluded

	Balance Sheet				

This Page Not Used.

PROBLEM 1-5 ___

1.

		ASSETS						=	LIABILITIES	+	STOCKHOLDERS' EQUITY
		Accounts							Accounts		
Cash	+	Receivable	+	Supplies	+	Land		=	Payable	+	Common Stock + Retained Earnings
____	+	____	+	____	+	____		=	____	+	____ + Retained Earnings
								=		+ Retained Earnings	+ Retained Earnings
								=	Retained Earnings		

PROBLEM 1-5 _____, Continued

2.

	ASSETS			=	LIABILITIES +			STOCKHOLDERS' EQUITY								
Cash +	Accts. Rec. +	Supplies +	Land =		Accounts Payable +	Common Stock +	Retained Earnings –	Dividends +	Dry Cleaning Revenue –	Dry Cleaning Exp. –	Wages Exp. –	Rent Exp. –	Supp. Exp. –	Truck Exp. –	Util. Exp. –	Misc. Exp.	
Bal.																	
A.																	
Bal.																	
B.																	
Bal.																	
C.																	
Bal.																	
D.																	
Bal.																	
E.																	
Bal.																	
F.																	
Bal.																	
G.																	
Bal.																	
H.																	
Bal.																	
I.																	
Bal.																	
J.																	
Bal.																	
K.																	
Bal.																	
L.																	
Bal.																	

PROBLEM 1-5 ___, Continued

3.

Income Statement

Retained Earnings Statement

PROBLEM 1-5 ___, Continued

	Balance Sheet			

PROBLEM 1-5 ___, Concluded

4. (Optional)

Statement of Cash Flows

This Page Not Used.

PROBLEM 1-6 ___

A. _____

_____

B. _____

_____

C. _____

_____

D. _____

_____

E. _____

_____

F. _____

_____

G. _____

_____

H. _____

_____

I. _____

_____

J. _____

_____

K. _____

_____

L. _____

_____

M. _____

_____

N. _____

_____

O. _____

_____

P. _____

_____

Q. _____

_____

This Page Not Used.

CONTINUING PROBLEM

1.

	ASSETS			=	LIABILITIES +				STOCKHOLDERS' EQUITY							
	Cash +	Accts. Rec. +	Supplies =		Accounts Payable +	Common Stock −	Dividends +	Fees Earned −	Music Exp. −	Office Rent Exp. −	Equip. Rent Exp. −	Adv. Exp. −	Wages Exp. −	Util. Exp. −	Sup. Exp. −	Misc. Exp.
6/1																
6/2																
Bal.																
6/2																
Bal.																
6/2																
Bal.																
6/4																
Bal.																
6/6																
Bal.																
6/6																
Bal.																
6/8																
Bal.																
6/12																
Bal.																
6/13																
Bal.																
6/16																
Bal.																
6/22																
Bal.																
6/25																
Bal.																

Name _____

CONTINUING PROBLEM, Continued

	ASSETS			=	LIABILITIES	+	STOCKHOLDERS' EQUITY										
	Cash	+	Accts. Rec.	+ Supplies	=	Accounts Payable	+	Common Stock	− Dividends	+	Fees Earned	− Music Exp.	− Office Rent Exp.	− Equip. Rent Exp.	− Adv. Exp.	− Wages Exp.	− Util. Exp.	− Sup. Exp.	− Misc. Exp.
6/29																		
Bal.																		
6/30																		
Bal.																		
6/30																		
Bal.																		
6/30																		
Bal.																		
6/30																		
Bal.																		
6/30																		
Bal.																		
6/30																		
Bal.																		
6/30																		
Bal.																		

CONTINUING PROBLEM, Continued

2.

Income Statement

3.

Retained Earnings Statement

CONTINUING PROBLEM, Concluded

4.

	Balance Sheet		

EXERCISE 2-1

Accounts Payable: _____

Advanced Payments for Equipment: _____

Air Traffic Liability: _____

Aircraft Fuel (Expense): _____

Aircraft Maintenance (Expense): _____

Aircraft Rent (Expense): _____

Cargo Revenue: _____

Cash: _____

Contract Carrier Arrangements (Expense): _____

Flight Equipment: _____

Frequent Flyer (Obligations): _____

Fuel Inventory: _____

Landing Fees (Expense): _____

Parts and Supplies Inventories: _____

Passenger Commissions (Expense): _____

Passenger Revenue: _____

Prepaid Expenses: _____

Taxes Payable: _____

EXERCISE 2-2

Account	Account Number
Accounts Payable..................	_____
Accounts Receivable.............	_____
Cash	_____
Common Stock......................	_____
Dividends..............................	_____
Fees Earned.........................	_____
Land ….............................…	_____
Miscellaneous Expense	_____
Retained Earnings.................	_____
Supplies Expense ….............	_____
Wages Expense	_____

EXERCISE 2-3

Balance Sheet Accounts	
Acct. #	Account Name
	1. Assets
	2. Liabilities
	3. Stockholders' Equity

Income Statement Accounts	
Acct. #	Account Name
	4. Revenue
	5. Expenses

EXERCISE 2-4

	Increase	Decrease	Normal Balance
Balance sheet accounts:			
Asset	A. _____	B. _____	Debit
Liability	C. _____	Debit	D. _____
Stockholders' Equity:			
Common Stock	Credit	E. _____	F. _____
Retained Earnings	G. _____	H. _____	Credit
Dividends	Debit	Credit	I. _____
Income statement accounts:			
Revenue	J. _____	K. _____	Credit
Expense	L. _____	Credit	Debit

EXERCISE 2-5

1. Accounts Payable: _____

2. Accounts Receivable: _____

3. Cash: _____

4. Fees Earned: _____

5. Insurance Expense: _____

6. Dividends: _____

7. Utilities Expense: _____

EXERCISE 2-6

A. Accounts Payable: _____

B. Accounts Receivable: _____

C. Cash: _____

D. Common Stock: _____

E. Dividends: _____

F. Fees Earned: _____

G. Office Equipment: _____

H. Rent Expense: _____

I. Supplies: _____

J. Wages Expense: _____

EXERCISE 2-7

JOURNAL

	DATE		DESCRIPTION	POST. REF.	DEBIT	CREDIT	
1							1
2							2
3							3
4							4
5							5
6							6
7							7
8							8
9							9
10							10
11							11
12							12
13							13
14							14
15							15
16							16
17							17
18							18
19							19
20							20
21							21
22							22
23							23
24							24
25							25
26							26
27							27
28							28
29							29
30							30
31							31
32							32
33							33
34							34
35							35
36							36

EXERCISE 2-8

A.

JOURNAL   PAGE *33*

	DATE		DESCRIPTION	POST. REF.	DEBIT	CREDIT	
1							1
2							2
3							3
4							4
5							5

B., C., and D.

ACCOUNT   ACCOUNT NO. _____

	DATE		ITEM	POST. REF.	DEBIT	CREDIT	BALANCE DEBIT	BALANCE CREDIT	

ACCOUNT   ACCOUNT NO. _____

	DATE		ITEM	POST. REF.	DEBIT	CREDIT	BALANCE DEBIT	BALANCE CREDIT	

E. _____

EXERCISE 2-9

A.

		JOURNAL				PAGE

	DATE		DESCRIPTION	POST. REF.	DEBIT	CREDIT	
1							1
2							2
3							3
4							4
5							5
6							6
7							7
8							8
9							9
10							10
11							11
12							12

B.

Cash

_____|_____

_____|_____

Supplies

_____|_____

_____|_____

Accounts Receivable

_____|_____

_____|_____

Accounts Payable

_____|_____

_____|_____

Fees Earned

_____|_____

_____|_____

C. _____

_____

_____

_____

_____

_____

_____

EXERCISE 2-10

A. _____

_____

_____

_____

_____

B. _____

_____

EXERCISE 2-11

A.

Accounts Payable

B.

Accounts Receivable

EXERCISE 2-11, Concluded

C.

Cash

EXERCISE 2-12

A. _____

_____

_____

_____

B. _____

_____

_____

_____

EXERCISE 2-13

A. and B.

Transaction	Account Debited Type	Effect	Account Credited Type	Effect
(1)	asset	+	stockholders' equity	+
(2)				
(3)				
(4)				
(5)				
(6)				
(7)				
(8)				
(9)				

EXERCISE 2-14

JOURNAL   PAGE

	DATE		DESCRIPTION	POST. REF.	DEBIT	CREDIT	
1							1
2							2
3							3
4							4
5							5
6							6
7							7
8							8
9							9
10							10
11							11
12							12
13							13
14							14
15							15
16							16
17							17
18							18
19							19
20							20
21							21
22							22
23							23
24							24
25							25
26							26
27							27
28							28
29							29
30							30
31							31
32							32
33							33
34							34
35							35
36							36

EXERCISE 2-15

A.

	Unadjusted Trial Balance		

B. _____

EXERCISE 2-16

	Unadjusted Trial Balance		

EXERCISE 2-17

EXERCISE 2-18

Unadjusted Trial Balance		

EXERCISE 2-19

Error	(A) Out of Balance	(B) Difference	(C) Larger Total
1.	yes	$6,000	debit
2.			
3.			
4.			
5.			
6.			
7.			

EXERCISE 2-20

_____

_____

_____

_____

_____

_____

_____

_____

_____

_____

_____

_____

(Optional)

_____

Unadjusted Trial Balance

_____

EXERCISE 2-21

JOURNAL

PAGE _____

	DATE	DESCRIPTION	POST. REF.	DEBIT	CREDIT	
1						1
2						2
3						3
4						4
5						5
6						6
7						7
8						8
9						9

EXERCISE 2-22

JOURNAL

PAGE _____

	DATE	DESCRIPTION	POST. REF.	DEBIT	CREDIT	
1						1
2						2
3						3
4						4
5						5
6						6
7						7
8						8
9						9
10						10

This Page Not Used.

PROBLEM 2-1 ___

1. and 2.

Cash

Accounts Receivable

Supplies

Prepaid Insurance

Automobiles

PROBLEM 2-1 ___ , Continued

Equipment

_____|_____
_____|_____
_____|_____

Notes Payable

_____|_____
_____|_____
_____|_____

Accounts Payable

_____|_____
_____|_____
_____|_____
_____|_____

Common Stock

_____|_____
_____|_____

Professional Fees

_____|_____
_____|_____
_____|_____
_____|_____

Rent Expense

_____|_____
_____|_____

PROBLEM 2-1 ___, Continued

Salary Expense

_____ | _____
_____ | _____

Blueprint Expense

_____ | _____
_____ | _____

Automobile Expense

_____ | _____
_____ | _____

Miscellaneous Expense

_____ | _____
_____ | _____
_____ | _____
_____ | _____

PROBLEM 2-1 ___ , Concluded

3.

Unadjusted Trial Balance		

4. _____

_____

PROBLEM 2-2 ___

1.

JOURNAL   PAGE

	DATE		DESCRIPTION	POST. REF.	DEBIT	CREDIT	
1							1
2							2
3							3
4							4
5							5
6							6
7							7
8							8
9							9
10							10
11							11
12							12
13							13
14							14
15							15
16							16
17							17
18							18
19							19
20							20
21							21
22							22
23							23
24							24
25							25
26							26
27							27
28							28
29							29
30							30
31							31
32							32
33							33
34							34
35							35

PROBLEM 2-2 ___, Continued

2.

Cash

Supplies

Accounts Payable

Common Stock

Dividends

Sales Commissions

PROBLEM 2-2 ___, Continued

Rent Expense

_____ | _____
_____ | _____

Office Salaries Expense

_____ | _____
_____ | _____

Automobile Expense

_____ | _____
_____ | _____

Supplies Expense

_____ | _____
_____ | _____

Miscellaneous Expense

_____ | _____
_____ | _____

PROBLEM 2-2 ___, Concluded

3.

	Unadjusted Trial Balance	

4. A. _____

   B. _____

   C. _____

5. _____

_____

PROBLEM 2-3 ___

1.

JOURNAL   PAGE *1*

	DATE	DESCRIPTION	POST. REF.	DEBIT	CREDIT	
1						1
2						2
3						3
4						4
5						5
6						6
7						7
8						8
9						9
10						10
11						11
12						12
13						13
14						14
15						15
16						16
17						17
18						18
19						19
20						20
21						21
22						22
23						23
24						24
25						25
26						26
27						27
28						28
29						29
30						30
31						31
32						32
33						33
34						34
35						35

PROBLEM 2-3 ___, Continued

JOURNAL

	DATE	DESCRIPTION	POST. REF.	DEBIT	CREDIT	
1						1
2						2
3						3
4						4
5						5
6						6
7						7
8						8
9						9
10						10
11						11
12						12
13						13
14						14
15						15
16						16
17						17
18						18
19						19
20						20
21						21
22						22
23						23
24						24
25						25
26						26
27						27
28						28
29						29
30						30
31						31
32						32
33						33
34						34
35						35
36						36

PROBLEM 2-3 ___, Continued

2.

GENERAL LEDGER

ACCOUNT   *Cash*   ACCOUNT NO.   11

DATE	ITEM	POST. REF.	DEBIT	CREDIT	BALANCE	
					DEBIT	CREDIT

ACCOUNT   *Accounts Receivable*   ACCOUNT NO.   12

DATE	ITEM	POST. REF.	DEBIT	CREDIT	BALANCE	
					DEBIT	CREDIT

ACCOUNT   *Supplies*   ACCOUNT NO.   13

DATE	ITEM	POST. REF.	DEBIT	CREDIT	BALANCE	
					DEBIT	CREDIT

ACCOUNT   *Prepaid Insurance*   ACCOUNT NO.   14

DATE	ITEM	POST. REF.	DEBIT	CREDIT	BALANCE	
					DEBIT	CREDIT

PROBLEM 2-3 ___, Continued

ACCOUNT   *Equipment*   ACCOUNT NO. 16

DATE		ITEM	POST. REF.	DEBIT	CREDIT	BALANCE	
						DEBIT	CREDIT

ACCOUNT   *Truck*   ACCOUNT NO. 18

DATE		ITEM	POST. REF.	DEBIT	CREDIT	BALANCE	
						DEBIT	CREDIT

ACCOUNT   *Notes Payable*   ACCOUNT NO. 21

DATE		ITEM	POST. REF.	DEBIT	CREDIT	BALANCE	
						DEBIT	CREDIT

ACCOUNT   *Accounts Payable*   ACCOUNT NO. 22

DATE		ITEM	POST. REF.	DEBIT	CREDIT	BALANCE	
						DEBIT	CREDIT

ACCOUNT   *Common Stock*   ACCOUNT NO. 31

DATE		ITEM	POST. REF.	DEBIT	CREDIT	BALANCE	
						DEBIT	CREDIT

PROBLEM 2-3 ___, Continued

ACCOUNT   *Dividends*   ACCOUNT NO. *33*

DATE		ITEM	POST. REF.	DEBIT	CREDIT	BALANCE	
						DEBIT	CREDIT

ACCOUNT   *Fees Earned*   ACCOUNT NO. *41*

DATE		ITEM	POST. REF.	DEBIT	CREDIT	BALANCE	
						DEBIT	CREDIT

ACCOUNT   *Wages Expense*   ACCOUNT NO. *51*

DATE		ITEM	POST. REF.	DEBIT	CREDIT	BALANCE	
						DEBIT	CREDIT

ACCOUNT   *Rent Expense*   ACCOUNT NO. *53*

DATE		ITEM	POST. REF.	DEBIT	CREDIT	BALANCE	
						DEBIT	CREDIT

ACCOUNT   *Utilities Expense*   ACCOUNT NO. *54*

DATE		ITEM	POST. REF.	DEBIT	CREDIT	BALANCE	
						DEBIT	CREDIT

PROBLEM 2-3 ___ , Continued

ACCOUNT   *Truck Expense*   ACCOUNT NO. 55

DATE		ITEM	POST. REF.	DEBIT	CREDIT	BALANCE	
						DEBIT	CREDIT

ACCOUNT   *Miscellaneous Expense*   ACCOUNT NO. 59

DATE		ITEM	POST. REF.	DEBIT	CREDIT	BALANCE	
						DEBIT	CREDIT

PROBLEM 2-3 ___, Concluded

3.

Unadjusted Trial Balance			

4. _____

_____

5. _____

_____

_____

_____

_____

_____

_____

This Page Not Used.

PROBLEM 2-4 ___

2. and 3.

JOURNAL   PAGE *18*

	DATE		DESCRIPTION	POST. REF.	DEBIT	CREDIT	
1							1
2							2
3							3
4							4
5							5
6							6
7							7
8							8
9							9
10							10
11							11
12							12
13							13
14							14
15							15
16							16
17							17
18							18
19							19
20							20
21							21
22							22
23							23
24							24
25							25
26							26
27							27
28							28
29							29
30							30
31							31
32							32
33							33
34							34
35							35

PROBLEM 2-4 ___, Continued

JOURNAL

	DATE		DESCRIPTION	POST. REF.	DEBIT	CREDIT	
1							1
2							2
3							3
4							4
5							5
6							6
7							7
8							8
9							9
10							10
11							11
12							12
13							13
14							14
15							15
16							16
17							17
18							18
19							19
20							20
21							21
22							22
23							23
24							24
25							25
26							26
27							27
28							28
29							29
30							30
31							31
32							32
33							33
34							34
35							35
36							36

PROBLEM 2-4 ___, Continued

1. and 3.

GENERAL LEDGER

ACCOUNT   *Cash*   ACCOUNT NO. *11*

DATE		ITEM	POST. REF.	DEBIT	CREDIT	BALANCE	
						DEBIT	CREDIT

ACCOUNT   *Accounts Receivable*   ACCOUNT NO. *12*

DATE		ITEM	POST. REF.	DEBIT	CREDIT	BALANCE	
						DEBIT	CREDIT

ACCOUNT   *Prepaid Insurance*   ACCOUNT NO. *13*

DATE		ITEM	POST. REF.	DEBIT	CREDIT	BALANCE	
						DEBIT	CREDIT

PROBLEM 2-4 ___ , Continued

ACCOUNT   *Office Supplies*   ACCOUNT NO. *14*

DATE	ITEM	POST. REF.	DEBIT	CREDIT	BALANCE	
					DEBIT	CREDIT

ACCOUNT   *Land*   ACCOUNT NO. *16*

DATE	ITEM	POST. REF.	DEBIT	CREDIT	BALANCE	
					DEBIT	CREDIT

ACCOUNT   *Accounts Payable*   ACCOUNT NO. *21*

DATE	ITEM	POST. REF.	DEBIT	CREDIT	BALANCE	
					DEBIT	CREDIT

ACCOUNT   *Unearned Rent*   ACCOUNT NO. *22*

DATE	ITEM	POST. REF.	DEBIT	CREDIT	BALANCE	
					DEBIT	CREDIT

ACCOUNT   *Notes Payable*   ACCOUNT NO. *23*

DATE	ITEM	POST. REF.	DEBIT	CREDIT	BALANCE	
					DEBIT	CREDIT

PROBLEM 2-4 ___, Continued

ACCOUNT *Common Stock*   ACCOUNT NO. 31

DATE		ITEM	POST. REF.	DEBIT	CREDIT	BALANCE DEBIT	BALANCE CREDIT

ACCOUNT *Retained Earnings*   ACCOUNT NO. 32

DATE		ITEM	POST. REF.	DEBIT	CREDIT	BALANCE DEBIT	BALANCE CREDIT

ACCOUNT *Dividends*   ACCOUNT NO. 33

DATE		ITEM	POST. REF.	DEBIT	CREDIT	BALANCE DEBIT	BALANCE CREDIT

ACCOUNT *Fees Earned*   ACCOUNT NO. 41

DATE		ITEM	POST. REF.	DEBIT	CREDIT	BALANCE DEBIT	BALANCE CREDIT

ACCOUNT *Salary and Commission Expense*   ACCOUNT NO. 51

DATE		ITEM	POST. REF.	DEBIT	CREDIT	BALANCE DEBIT	BALANCE CREDIT

PROBLEM 2-4 ___ , Continued

ACCOUNT   *Rent Expense*   ACCOUNT NO. 52

DATE		ITEM	POST. REF.	DEBIT	CREDIT	BALANCE	
						DEBIT	CREDIT

ACCOUNT   *Advertising Expense*   ACCOUNT NO. 53

DATE		ITEM	POST. REF.	DEBIT	CREDIT	BALANCE	
						DEBIT	CREDIT

ACCOUNT   *Automobile Expense*   ACCOUNT NO. 54

DATE		ITEM	POST. REF.	DEBIT	CREDIT	BALANCE	
						DEBIT	CREDIT

ACCOUNT   *Miscellaneous Expense*   ACCOUNT NO. 59

DATE		ITEM	POST. REF.	DEBIT	CREDIT	BALANCE	
						DEBIT	CREDIT

PROBLEM 2-4 ___, Concluded

4.

Unadjusted Trial Balance

5. A. _____

_____

B.

JOURNAL   PAGE

	DATE	DESCRIPTION	POST. REF.	DEBIT	CREDIT	
1						1
2						2
3						3
4						4

C. _____

This Page Not Used.

PROBLEM 2-5 ___

1.

Corrected Unadjusted Trial Balance	DEBIT BALANCES	CREDIT BALANCES
Cash		
Accounts Receivable		
Supplies		
Prepaid Insurance		
Equipment		
Notes Payable		
Accounts Payable		
Common Stock		
Retained Earnings		
Dividends		
Fees Earned		
Wages Expense		
Rent Expense		
Advertising Expense		
Gas, Electricity, and Water Expense		
Miscellaneous Expense		

2. _____

_____

_____

_____

_____

This Page Not Used.

CONTINUING PROBLEM

2. and 3.

JOURNAL

PAGE *1*

	DATE		DESCRIPTION	POST. REF.	DEBIT	CREDIT	
1							1
2							2
3							3
4							4
5							5
6							6
7							7
8							8
9							9
10							10
11							11
12							12
13							13
14							14
15							15
16							16
17							17
18							18
19							19
20							20
21							21
22							22
23							23
24							24
25							25
26							26
27							27
28							28
29							29
30							30
31							31
32							32
33							33
34							34
35							35

CONTINUING PROBLEM, Continued

JOURNAL

	DATE		DESCRIPTION	POST. REF.	DEBIT	CREDIT	
1							1
2							2
3							3
4							4
5							5
6							6
7							7
8							8
9							9
10							10
11							11
12							12
13							13
14							14
15							15
16							16
17							17
18							18
19							19
20							20
21							21
22							22
23							23
24							24
25							25
26							26
27							27
28							28
29							29
30							30
31							31
32							32
33							33
34							34
35							35
36							36

CONTINUING PROBLEM, Continued

JOURNAL

	DATE		DESCRIPTION	POST. REF.	DEBIT	CREDIT	
1							1
2							2
3							3
4							4
5							5
6							6
7							7
8							8
9							9
10							10
11							11
12							12
13							13
14							14
15							15
16							16
17							17
18							18
19							19
20							20
21							21
22							22
23							23
24							24
25							25
26							26
27							27
28							28
29							29
30							30
31							31
32							32
33							33
34							34
35							35
36							36

CONTINUING PROBLEM, Continued

1. and 3.

GENERAL LEDGER

ACCOUNT   *Cash*   ACCOUNT NO.   *11*

DATE		ITEM	POST. REF.	DEBIT	CREDIT	BALANCE	
						DEBIT	CREDIT

CONTINUING PROBLEM, Continued

ACCOUNT   *Accounts Receivable*   ACCOUNT NO. 12

DATE		ITEM	POST. REF.	DEBIT	CREDIT	BALANCE	
						DEBIT	CREDIT

ACCOUNT   *Supplies*   ACCOUNT NO. 14

DATE		ITEM	POST. REF.	DEBIT	CREDIT	BALANCE	
						DEBIT	CREDIT

ACCOUNT   *Prepaid Insurance*   ACCOUNT NO. 15

DATE		ITEM	POST. REF.	DEBIT	CREDIT	BALANCE	
						DEBIT	CREDIT

ACCOUNT   *Office Equipment*   ACCOUNT NO. 17

DATE		ITEM	POST. REF.	DEBIT	CREDIT	BALANCE	
						DEBIT	CREDIT

CONTINUING PROBLEM, Continued

ACCOUNT *Accumulated Depreciation—Office Equipment* ACCOUNT NO. *18*

DATE		ITEM	POST. REF.	DEBIT	CREDIT	BALANCE	
						DEBIT	CREDIT

(This account is not used in Chapter 2.)

ACCOUNT *Accounts Payable* ACCOUNT NO. *21*

DATE		ITEM	POST. REF.	DEBIT	CREDIT	BALANCE	
						DEBIT	CREDIT

ACCOUNT *Wages Payable* ACCOUNT NO. *22*

DATE		ITEM	POST. REF.	DEBIT	CREDIT	BALANCE	
						DEBIT	CREDIT

(This account is not used in Chapter 2.)

ACCOUNT *Unearned Revenue* ACCOUNT NO. *23*

DATE		ITEM	POST. REF.	DEBIT	CREDIT	BALANCE	
						DEBIT	CREDIT

CONTINUING PROBLEM, Continued

ACCOUNT *Common Stock*   ACCOUNT NO. *31*

DATE		ITEM	POST. REF.	DEBIT	CREDIT	BALANCE	
						DEBIT	CREDIT

ACCOUNT *Dividends*   ACCOUNT NO. *33*

DATE		ITEM	POST. REF.	DEBIT	CREDIT	BALANCE	
						DEBIT	CREDIT

ACCOUNT *Fees Earned*   ACCOUNT NO. *41*

DATE		ITEM	POST. REF.	DEBIT	CREDIT	BALANCE	
						DEBIT	CREDIT

CONTINUING PROBLEM, Continued

ACCOUNT   *Wages Expense*   ACCOUNT NO. *50*

DATE		ITEM	POST. REF.	DEBIT	CREDIT	BALANCE	
						DEBIT	CREDIT

ACCOUNT   *Office Rent Expense*   ACCOUNT NO. *51*

DATE		ITEM	POST. REF.	DEBIT	CREDIT	BALANCE	
						DEBIT	CREDIT

ACCOUNT   *Equipment Rent Expense*   ACCOUNT NO. *52*

DATE		ITEM	POST. REF.	DEBIT	CREDIT	BALANCE	
						DEBIT	CREDIT

ACCOUNT   *Utilities Expense*   ACCOUNT NO. *53*

DATE		ITEM	POST. REF.	DEBIT	CREDIT	BALANCE	
						DEBIT	CREDIT

CONTINUING PROBLEM, Continued

ACCOUNT   *Music Expense*   ACCOUNT NO. 54

DATE		ITEM	POST. REF.	DEBIT	CREDIT	BALANCE	
						DEBIT	CREDIT

ACCOUNT   *Advertising Expense*   ACCOUNT NO. 55

DATE		ITEM	POST. REF.	DEBIT	CREDIT	BALANCE	
						DEBIT	CREDIT

ACCOUNT   *Supplies Expense*   ACCOUNT NO. 56

DATE		ITEM	POST. REF.	DEBIT	CREDIT	BALANCE	
						DEBIT	CREDIT

ACCOUNT   *Insurance Expense*   ACCOUNT NO. 57

DATE		ITEM	POST. REF.	DEBIT	CREDIT	BALANCE	
						DEBIT	CREDIT

(This account is not used in Chapter 2.)

CONTINUING PROBLEM, Continued

ACCOUNT   *Depreciation Expense*   ACCOUNT NO. 58

DATE	ITEM	POST. REF.	DEBIT	CREDIT	BALANCE DEBIT	BALANCE CREDIT

(This account is not used in Chapter 2.)

ACCOUNT   *Miscellaneous Expense*   ACCOUNT NO. 59

DATE	ITEM	POST. REF.	DEBIT	CREDIT	BALANCE DEBIT	BALANCE CREDIT

CONTINUING PROBLEM, Concluded

4.

	Unadjusted Trial Balance		

This Page Not Used.

EXERCISE 3-1

1. A two-year premium paid on a fire insurance policy: _____

2. Fees earned but not yet received: _____

3. Fees received but not yet earned: _____

4. Salary owed but not yet paid: _____

5. Subscriptions received in advance by a magazine publisher: _____

6. Supplies on hand: _____

7. Taxes owed but payable in the following period: _____

8. Utilities owed but not yet paid: _____

EXERCISE 3-2

Account	Answer
Accounts Receivable	Normally requires adjustment (AR).
Cash...	
Common Stock	
Interest Expense......................	
Interest Receivable	
Land	
Office Equipment	
Prepaid Rent............................	
Supplies	
Unearned Fees	
Wages Expense.......................	

EXERCISE 3-3

A.

JOURNAL

PAGE _____

	DATE		DESCRIPTION	POST. REF.	DEBIT	CREDIT	
1							1
2							2
3							3
4							4

B. _____

_____

_____

_____

_____

_____

EXERCISE 3-4

A. _____

_____

B. _____

_____

EXERCISE 3-5

A. and B.

JOURNAL

PAGE _____

	DATE		DESCRIPTION	POST. REF.	DEBIT	CREDIT	
1							1
2							2
3							3
4							4
5							5
6							6
7							7
8							8
9							9
10							10

EXERCISE 3-6

_____

EXERCISE 3-7

A. _____

_____

_____

B. _____

_____

_____

EXERCISE 3-8

A. _____

_____

B. _____

_____

_____

_____

_____

EXERCISE 3-9

JOURNAL

PAGE

	DATE		DESCRIPTION	POST. REF.	DEBIT	CREDIT	
1							1
2							2
3							3
4							4

EXERCISE 3-10

A. _____

_____

_____

B. _____

_____

_____

EXERCISE 3-11

JOURNAL   PAGE

	DATE		DESCRIPTION	POST. REF.	DEBIT	CREDIT	
1							1
2							2
3							3
4							4

EXERCISE 3-12

_____

EXERCISE 3-13

A. _____

_____

_____

B. _____

_____

_____

EXERCISE 3-14

A. and B.

JOURNAL   PAGE

	DATE		DESCRIPTION	POST. REF.	DEBIT	CREDIT	
1							1
2							2
3							3
4							4
5							5
6							6
7							7
8							8

EXERCISE 3-15

A. and B.

JOURNAL

PAGE _____

	DATE		DESCRIPTION	POST. REF.	DEBIT	CREDIT	
1							1
2							2
3							3
4							4
5							5
6							6
7							7
8							8

EXERCISE 3-16

A. and B.

JOURNAL

PAGE _____

	DATE		DESCRIPTION	POST. REF.	DEBIT	CREDIT	
1							1
2							2
3							3
4							4
5							5
6							6
7							7
8							8

EXERCISE 3-17

A.

JOURNAL   PAGE

	DATE		DESCRIPTION	POST. REF.	DEBIT	CREDIT	
1							1
2							2
3							3
4							4
5							5
6							6
7							7
8							8
9							9
10							10

B. _____

EXERCISE 3-18

JOURNAL   PAGE

	DATE		DESCRIPTION	POST. REF.	DEBIT	CREDIT	
1							1
2							2
3							3
4							4

EXERCISE 3-19

A. _____

B. _____

_____

_____

EXERCISE 3-20

A. _____

B. _____

_____

_____

_____

_____

EXERCISE 3-21

_____

EXERCISE 3-22

A. _____

B. _____

EXERCISE 3-23

	Error (A)		Error (B)	
	Overstated	Understated	Overstated	Understated
1. Revenue for the year would be...............	$	$	$	$
2. Expenses for the year would be	$	$	$	$
3. Net income for the year would be..........	$	$	$	$
4. Assets at July 31 would be	$	$	$	$
5. Liabilities at July 31 would be	$	$	$	$
6. Stockholders' equity at July 31 would be......	$	$	$	$

EXERCISE 3-24

_____

_____

EXERCISE 3-25

A.

JOURNAL   PAGE

	DATE		DESCRIPTION	POST. REF.	DEBIT	CREDIT	
1							1
2							2
3							3
4							4

B. (1) _____

_____

_____

(2) _____

_____

_____

EXERCISE 3-26

JOURNAL   PAGE

	DATE		DESCRIPTION	POST. REF.	DEBIT	CREDIT	
1							1
2							2
3							3
4							4
5							5
6							6
7							7
8							8
9							9
10							10
11							11
12							12
13							13
14							14
15							15
16							16
17							17
18							18
19							19
20							20
21							21
22							22

EXERCISE 3-27

_____
_____
_____
_____
_____
_____
_____
_____
_____
_____
_____
_____
_____
_____
_____
_____
_____
_____
_____
_____

EXERCISE 3-27, Concluded

(Optional)

	Adjusted Trial Balance	

PROBLEM 3-1 ___

1.

	DATE		DESCRIPTION	POST. REF.	DEBIT	CREDIT	
1							1
2							2
3							3
4							4
5							5
6							6
7							7
8							8
9							9
10							10
11							11
12							12
13							13
14							14
15							15
16							16
17							17
18							18
19							19
20							20
21							21
22							22
23							23
24							24

JOURNAL   PAGE

2. _____

_____

_____

_____

_____

This Page Not Used.

PROBLEM 3-2 ___

1.

JOURNAL

PAGE ____

	DATE		DESCRIPTION	POST. REF.	DEBIT	CREDIT	
1							1
2							2
3							3
4							4
5							5
6							6
7							7
8							8
9							9
10							10
11							11
12							12
13							13
14							14
15							15
16							16
17							17
18							18
19							19
20							20
21							21
22							22
23							23
24							24
25							25
26							26
27							27
28							28
29							29
30							30
31							31
32							32
33							33
34							34
35							35

PROBLEM 3-2 ___, Concluded

2. _____

_____

_____

_____

3. _____

_____

_____

_____

_____

_____

_____

_____

_____

_____

_____

_____

4. _____

_____

_____

_____

PROBLEM 3-3 ___

1.

JOURNAL

PAGE

	DATE		DESCRIPTION	POST. REF.	DEBIT	CREDIT	
1							1
2							2
3							3
4							4
5							5
6							6
7							7
8							8
9							9
10							10
11							11
12							12
13							13
14							14
15							15
16							16
17							17
18							18
19							19
20							20
21							21
22							22
23							23
24							24
25							25
26							26
27							27
28							28
29							29
30							30
31							31
32							32
33							33
34							34
35							35

PROBLEM 3-3 ___ , Concluded

2.

	AMOUNT	

3.

	AMOUNT	

4. _____

_____

_____

_____

PROBLEM 3-4 ___

JOURNAL

	DATE		DESCRIPTION	POST. REF.	DEBIT	CREDIT	
1							1
2							2
3							3
4							4
5							5
6							6
7							7
8							8
9							9
10							10
11							11
12							12
13							13
14							14
15							15
16							16
17							17
18							18
19							19
20							20
21							21
22							22
23							23
24							24
25							25
26							26
27							27
28							28
29							29
30							30
31							31
32							32
33							33
34							34
35							35
36							36

PROBLEM 3-4 ____, Concluded

JOURNAL

	DATE		DESCRIPTION	POST. REF.	DEBIT	CREDIT	
1							1
2							2
3							3
4							4
5							5
6							6
7							7
8							8
9							9
10							10
11							11
12							12
13							13
14							14
15							15
16							16
17							17
18							18
19							19
20							20
21							21
22							22
23							23
24							24
25							25
26							26
27							27
28							28
29							29
30							30
31							31
32							32
33							33
34							34
35							35
36							36

PROBLEM 3-5 ___

1.

JOURNAL   PAGE

	DATE		DESCRIPTION	POST. REF.	DEBIT	CREDIT	
1							1
2							2
3							3
4							4
5							5
6							6
7							7
8							8
9							9
10							10
11							11
12							12
13							13
14							14
15							15
16							16
17							17
18							18
19							19
20							20
21							21
22							22
23							23
24							24
25							25
26							26
27							27
28							28
29							29
30							30
31							31
32							32
33							33
34							34
35							35

PROBLEM 3-5 ___, Concluded

2.

	Adjusted Trial Balance		

PROBLEM 3-6 ___

1.

					POST. REF.	DEBIT	CREDIT	
	DATE		DESCRIPTION					
1								1
2								2
3								3
4								4
5								5
6								6
7								7
8								8
9								9
10								10
11								11
12								12
13								13
14								14
15								15
16								16
17								17
18								18
19								19
20								20

JOURNAL   PAGE

2.

	Net Income	Total Assets	=	Total Liabilities	+	Total Stockholders' Equity
Reported amounts	$ _____	$ _____		$ _____		$ _____
Corrections:						
Adjustment (a)	_____	_____		_____		_____
Adjustment (b)	_____	_____		_____		_____
Adjustment (c)	_____	_____		_____		_____
Adjustment (d)	_____	_____		_____		_____
Corrected amounts	$ _____	$ _____		$ _____		$ _____

This Page Not Used.

CONTINUING PROBLEM

1.

JOURNAL PAGE 3

	DATE		DESCRIPTION	POST. REF.	DEBIT	CREDIT	
1							1
2							2
3							3
4							4
5							5
6							6
7							7
8							8
9							9
10							10
11							11
12							12
13							13
14							14
15							15
16							16
17							17
18							18
19							19
20							20
21							21
22							22
23							23
24							24
25							25
26							26
27							27
28							28
29							29
30							30
31							31
32							32
33							33
34							34
35							35

CONTINUING PROBLEM, Continued

2.

GENERAL LEDGER

ACCOUNT   *Cash*   ACCOUNT NO. *11*

DATE		ITEM	POST. REF.	DEBIT	CREDIT	BALANCE	
						DEBIT	CREDIT

CONTINUING PROBLEM, Continued

ACCOUNT *Accounts Receivable*   ACCOUNT NO. *12*

DATE		ITEM	POST. REF.	DEBIT	CREDIT	BALANCE	
						DEBIT	CREDIT

ACCOUNT *Supplies*   ACCOUNT NO. *14*

DATE		ITEM	POST. REF.	DEBIT	CREDIT	BALANCE	
						DEBIT	CREDIT

ACCOUNT *Prepaid Insurance*   ACCOUNT NO. *15*

DATE		ITEM	POST. REF.	DEBIT	CREDIT	BALANCE	
						DEBIT	CREDIT

ACCOUNT *Office Equipment*   ACCOUNT NO. *17*

DATE		ITEM	POST. REF.	DEBIT	CREDIT	BALANCE	
						DEBIT	CREDIT

CONTINUING PROBLEM, Continued

ACCOUNT   *Accumulated Depreciation—Office Equipment*   ACCOUNT NO. 18

DATE		ITEM	POST. REF.	DEBIT	CREDIT	BALANCE	
						DEBIT	CREDIT

ACCOUNT   *Accounts Payable*   ACCOUNT NO. 21

DATE		ITEM	POST. REF.	DEBIT	CREDIT	BALANCE	
						DEBIT	CREDIT

ACCOUNT   *Wages Payable*   ACCOUNT NO. 22

DATE		ITEM	POST. REF.	DEBIT	CREDIT	BALANCE	
						DEBIT	CREDIT

ACCOUNT   *Unearned Revenue*   ACCOUNT NO. 23

DATE		ITEM	POST. REF.	DEBIT	CREDIT	BALANCE	
						DEBIT	CREDIT

CONTINUING PROBLEM, Continued

ACCOUNT *Common Stock* ACCOUNT NO. 31

DATE	ITEM	POST. REF.	DEBIT	CREDIT	BALANCE	
					DEBIT	CREDIT

ACCOUNT *Retained Earnings* ACCOUNT NO. 32

DATE	ITEM	POST. REF.	DEBIT	CREDIT	BALANCE	
					DEBIT	CREDIT

(This account is not used in Chapter 3.)

ACCOUNT *Dividends* ACCOUNT NO. 33

DATE	ITEM	POST. REF.	DEBIT	CREDIT	BALANCE	
					DEBIT	CREDIT

ACCOUNT *Income Summary* ACCOUNT NO. 34

DATE	ITEM	POST. REF.	DEBIT	CREDIT	BALANCE	
					DEBIT	CREDIT

(This account is not used in Chapter 3.)

CONTINUING PROBLEM, Continued

ACCOUNT   *Fees Earned*   ACCOUNT NO. *41*

DATE		ITEM	POST. REF.	DEBIT	CREDIT	BALANCE	
						DEBIT	CREDIT

ACCOUNT   *Wages Expense*   ACCOUNT NO. *50*

DATE		ITEM	POST. REF.	DEBIT	CREDIT	BALANCE	
						DEBIT	CREDIT

ACCOUNT   *Office Rent Expense*   ACCOUNT NO. *51*

DATE		ITEM	POST. REF.	DEBIT	CREDIT	BALANCE	
						DEBIT	CREDIT

CONTINUING PROBLEM, Continued

ACCOUNT   *Equipment Rent Expense*   ACCOUNT NO. **52**

DATE		ITEM	POST. REF.	DEBIT	CREDIT	BALANCE	
						DEBIT	CREDIT

ACCOUNT   *Utilities Expense*   ACCOUNT NO. **53**

DATE		ITEM	POST. REF.	DEBIT	CREDIT	BALANCE	
						DEBIT	CREDIT

ACCOUNT   *Music Expense*   ACCOUNT NO. **54**

DATE		ITEM	POST. REF.	DEBIT	CREDIT	BALANCE	
						DEBIT	CREDIT

ACCOUNT   *Advertising Expense*   ACCOUNT NO. **55**

DATE		ITEM	POST. REF.	DEBIT	CREDIT	BALANCE	
						DEBIT	CREDIT

CONTINUING PROBLEM, Continued

ACCOUNT *Supplies Expense*   ACCOUNT NO. 56

DATE		ITEM	POST. REF.	DEBIT	CREDIT	BALANCE	
						DEBIT	CREDIT

ACCOUNT *Insurance Expense*   ACCOUNT NO. 57

DATE		ITEM	POST. REF.	DEBIT	CREDIT	BALANCE	
						DEBIT	CREDIT

ACCOUNT *Depreciation Expense*   ACCOUNT NO. 58

DATE		ITEM	POST. REF.	DEBIT	CREDIT	BALANCE	
						DEBIT	CREDIT

ACCOUNT *Miscellaneous Expense*   ACCOUNT NO. 59

DATE		ITEM	POST. REF.	DEBIT	CREDIT	BALANCE	
						DEBIT	CREDIT

CONTINUING PROBLEM, Concluded

3.

	Adjusted Trial Balance		

This Page Not Used.

EXERCISE 4-1

1. Accounts Payable: _____
2. Accounts Receivable: _____
3. Cash: _____
4. Dividends: _____
5. Fees Earned: _____
6. Supplies: _____
7. Unearned Rent: _____
8. Utilities Expense: _____
9. Wages Expense: _____
10. Wages Payable: _____

EXERCISE 4-2

1. Accounts Receivable: _____
2. Equipment: _____
3. Fees Earned: _____
4. Insurance Expense: _____
5. Prepaid Advertising: _____
6. Prepaid Rent: _____
7. Rent Revenue: _____
8. Salary Expense: _____
9. Salary Payable: _____
10. Supplies: _____
11. Supplies Expense: _____
12. Unearned Rent: _____

EXERCISE 4-3

Income Statement		

Retained Earnings Statement		

EXERCISE 4-3, Concluded

	Balance Sheet		

EXERCISE 4-4

Income Statement

Retained Earnings Statement

EXERCISE 4-4, Concluded

	Balance Sheet		

EXERCISE 4-5

Income Statement		

EXERCISE 4-6

Income Statement		

EXERCISE 4-7

A.

	Income Statement		

B. _____

_____

_____

_____

_____

_____

_____

_____

_____

_____

EXERCISE 4-8

Retained Earnings Statement		

EXERCISE 4-9

Retained Earnings Statement		

EXERCISE 4-10

1. Accounts Receivable: _____
2. Building: _____
3. Cash: _____
4. Equipment: _____
5. Prepaid Insurance: _____
6. Supplies: _____

EXERCISE 4-11

_____

_____

_____

_____

_____

_____

_____

EXERCISE 4-12

	Balance Sheet			

EXERCISE 4-13

EXERCISE 4-13, Concluded

	Balance Sheet		

EXERCISE 4-14

A. Accounts Payable: _____

B. Accumulated Depreciation—Equipment: _____

C. Depreciation Expense—Equipment: _____

D. Equipment: _____

E. Common Stock: _____

F. Dividends: _____

G. Fees Earned: _____

H. Land: _____

 I. Supplies: _____

J. Supplies Expense: _____

K. Wages Expense: _____

L. Wages Payable: _____

EXERCISE 4-15

_____

_____

_____

_____

_____

_____

_____

_____

_____

EXERCISE 4-16

A.

JOURNAL   PAGE

	DATE		DESCRIPTION	POST. REF.	DEBIT	CREDIT	
1							1
2							2
3							3
4							4
5							5
6							6
7							7

B. _____

EXERCISE 4-17

		JOURNAL			PAGE	
	DATE	DESCRIPTION	POST. REF.	DEBIT	CREDIT	
1						1
2						2
3						3
4						4
5						5
6						6
7						7
8						8
9						9
10						10
11						11
12						12
13						13
14						14
15						15
16						16
17						17
18						18
19						19
20						20

EXERCISE 4-18

A. Accounts Payable: _____

B. Accumulated Depreciation: _____

C. Cash: _____

D. Common Stock: _____

E. Dividends: _____

F. Depreciation Expense: _____

G. Fees Earned: _____

H. Office Equipment: _____

I. Salaries Expense: _____

J. Salaries Payable: _____

K. Supplies: _____

EXERCISE 4-19

Post-Closing Trial Balance		

EXERCISE 4-20

1. _____   6. _____
2. _____   7. _____
3. _____   8. _____
4. _____   9. _____
5. _____   10. _____

APPENDIX 1 EXERCISE 4-21

1. _____   6. _____
2. _____   7. _____
3. _____   8. _____
4. _____   9. _____
5. _____   10. _____

APPENDIX 1 EXERCISE 4-22

Alert Security Services Co.
End-of-Period Spreadsheet (Work Sheet)
For the Year Ended October 31, 2018

	Unadjusted Trial Balance		Adjustments		Adjusted Trial Balance		Income Statement		Balance Sheet	
Account Title	Dr.	Cr.	Dr.	Cr.	Dr.	Cr.	Dr.	Cr.	Dr.	Cr.
Cash	12									
Accounts Receivable	90									
Supplies	8									
Prepaid Insurance	12									
Land	190									
Equipment	50									
Accumulated Depr.—Equip.		4								
Accounts Payable		36								
Wages Payable		0								
Common Stock		50								
Retained Earnings		210								
Dividends	8									
Fees Earned		200								
Wages Expense	110									
Rent Expense	12									
Insurance Expense	0									
Utilities Expense	6									
Supplies Expense	0									
Depr. Expense—Equipment	0									
Miscellaneous Expense	2									
Totals	500	500								

Alert Security Services Co.
End-of-Period Spreadsheet (Work Sheet)
For the Year Ended October 31, 2018

| | Unadjusted Trial Balance | | Adjustments | | Adjusted Trial Balance | | Income Statement | | Balance Sheet | |
Account Title	Dr.	Cr.	Dr.	Cr.	Dr.	Cr.	Dr.	Cr.	Dr.	Cr.
1										
2										
3										
4										
5										
6 Cash					12					
7 Accounts Receivable					103					
8 Supplies					4					
9 Prepaid Insurance					2					
10 Land					190					
11 Equipment					50					
12 Accumulated Depr.—Equip.						7				
13 Accounts Payable						36				
14 Wages Payable						1				
15 Common Stock						50				
16 Retained Earnings						210				
17 Dividends					8					
18 Fees Earned						213				
19 Wages Expense					111					
20 Rent Expense					12					
21 Insurance Expense					10					
22 Utilities Expense					6					
23 Supplies Expense					4					
24 Depr. Expense—Equipment					3					
25 Miscellaneous Expense					2					
26 Totals					517	517				
27 Net income (loss)										
28										

APPENDIX 1 EXERCISE 4-24

Income Statement

Retained Earnings Statement

APPENDIX 1 EXERCISE 4-24, Concluded

Balance Sheet

APPENDIX 1 EXERCISE 4-25

JOURNAL

PAGE

	DATE	DESCRIPTION	POST. REF.	DEBIT	CREDIT	
1						1
2						2
3						3
4						4
5						5
6						6
7						7
8						8
9						9
10						10
11						11
12						12
13						13
14						14
15						15
16						16
17						17
18						18
19						19
20						20
21						21
22						22
23						23
24						24

APPENDIX 1 EXERCISE 4-26

JOURNAL   PAGE ____

	DATE	DESCRIPTION	POST. REF.	DEBIT	CREDIT	
1						1
2						2
3						3
4						4
5						5
6						6
7						7
8						8
9						9
10						10
11						11
12						12
13						13
14						14
15						15
16						16
17						17
18						18
19						19
20						20
21						21
22						22
23						23
24						24

APPENDIX 2 EXERCISE 4-27

A., B., and C.

JOURNAL   PAGE

	DATE		DESCRIPTION	POST. REF.	DEBIT	CREDIT	
1							1
2							2
3							3
4							4
5							5
6							6
7							7
8							8
9							9
10							10

D. _____

APPENDIX 2 EXERCISE 4-28

A. and B.

JOURNAL   PAGE

	DATE		DESCRIPTION	POST. REF.	DEBIT	CREDIT	
1							1
2							2
3							3
4							4
5							5
6							6
7							7
8							8
9							9
10							10
11							11
12							12
13							13
14							14
15							15
16							16
17							17
18							18

APPENDIX 2 EXERCISE 4-29

A. and B.

JOURNAL   PAGE ____

	DATE		DESCRIPTION	POST. REF.	DEBIT	CREDIT	
1							1
2							2
3							3
4							4
5							5
6							6
7							7
8							8
9							9
10							10
11							11
12							12
13							13
14							14
15							15
16							16
17							17
18							18

APPENDIX 2 EXERCISE 4-30

A. (1) _____

 (2) _____

 (3) _____

 (4) _____

 (5) _____

B.

JOURNAL PAGE

	DATE		DESCRIPTION	POST. REF.	DEBIT	CREDIT	
1							1
2							2
3							3
4							4
5							5
6							6
7							7
8							8
9							9
10							10
11							11
12							12
13							13
14							14
15							15
16							16
17							17
18							18
19							19
20							20
21							21
22							22

APPENDIX 2 EXERCISE 4-31

A. (1) _____

(2) _____

(3) _____

(4) _____

(5) _____

B.

JOURNAL   PAGE

	DATE		DESCRIPTION	POST. REF.	DEBIT	CREDIT	
1							1
2							2
3							3
4							4
5							5
6							6
7							7
8							8
9							9
10							10
11							11
12							12
13							13
14							14
15							15
16							16
17							17
18							18
19							19
20							20
21							21
22							22

PROBLEM 4-1 ___

1.

Income Statement		

2.

Retained Earnings Statement		

PROBLEM 4-1 ___ , Continued

3.

	Balance Sheet			

PROBLEM 4-1 ___ , Continued

4.

JOURNAL   PAGE

	DATE		DESCRIPTION	POST. REF.	DEBIT	CREDIT	
1			*Closing Entries*				1
2							2
3							3
4							4
5							5
6							6
7							7
8							8
9							9
10							10
11							11
12							12
13							13
14							14
15							15
16							16
17							17
18							18
19							19
20							20
21							21
22							22
23							23
24							24
25							25
26							26
27							27
28							28
29							29
30							30
31							31
32							32
33							33
34							34
35							35

PROBLEM 4-1 ____, Concluded

5.

	Post-Closing Trial Balance		

PROBLEM 4-2 ___

1.

	Income Statement		

	Retained Earnings Statement		

PROBLEM 4-2 ___, Continued

Balance Sheet			

PROBLEM 4-2 ___ , Concluded

2.

JOURNAL   PAGE

	DATE		DESCRIPTION	POST. REF.	DEBIT	CREDIT	
1			*Closing Entries*				1
2							2
3							3
4							4
5							5
6							6
7							7
8							8
9							9
10							10
11							11
12							12
13							13
14							14
15							15
16							16
17							17
18							18
19							19
20							20
21							21
22							22
23							23
24							24

3. _____

_____

_____

_____

This Page Not Used.

PROBLEM 4-3 ___

1., 3., and 6.

Cash

Laundry Supplies

Prepaid Insurance

Laundry Equipment

Accumulated Depreciation

Accounts Payable

PROBLEM 4-3 ___, Continued

Wages Payable

Common Stock

Retained Earnings

Dividends

Income Summary

Laundry Revenue

PROBLEM 4-3 ___, Continued

Wages Expense

Rent Expense

Utilities Expense

Laundry Supplies Expense

Depreciation Expense

Insurance Expense

Miscellaneous Expense

Name _____

PROBLEM 4-3 _____, Continued

2. Optional (Appendix)

End-of-Period Spreadsheet (Work Sheet)

	A	B	C	D	E	F	G	H	I	J	K
	Account Title	Unadjusted Trial Balance		Adjustments		Adjusted Trial Balance		Income Statement		Balance Sheet	
		Dr.	Cr.	Dr.	Cr.	Dr.	Cr.	Dr.	Cr.	Dr.	Cr.
1											
2											
3											
4											
5											
6											
7											
8											
9											
10											
11											
12											
13											
14											
15											
16											
17											
18											
19											
20											
21											
22											
23											
24											
25											
26											
27											
28											
29											
30											

PROBLEM 4-3 ___ , Continued

3.

	DATE		DESCRIPTION	POST. REF.	DEBIT	CREDIT	
1			*Adjusting Entries*				1
2							2
3							3
4							4
5							5
6							6
7							7
8							8
9							9
10							10
11							11
12							12
13							13
14							14
15							15
16							16
17							17
18							18
19							19
20							20
21							21
22							22
23							23
24							24
25							25
26							26
27							27
28							28
29							29
30							30
31							31
32							32
33							33
34							34
35							35

JOURNAL   PAGE

PROBLEM 4-3 ___, Continued

4.

Adjusted Trial Balance		

PROBLEM 4-3 ___, Continued

5.

Income Statement		

Retained Earnings Statement		

PROBLEM 4-3 ___, Continued

	Balance Sheet			

PROBLEM 4-3 ___ , Continued

6.

		JOURNAL				PAGE

	DATE		DESCRIPTION	POST. REF.	DEBIT	CREDIT	
1			*Closing Entries*				1
2							2
3							3
4							4
5							5
6							6
7							7
8							8
9							9
10							10
11							11
12							12
13							13
14							14
15							15
16							16
17							17
18							18
19							19
20							20
21							21
22							22
23							23
24							24
25							25
26							26
27							27
28							28
29							29
30							30
31							31
32							32
33							33
34							34
35							35

PROBLEM 4-3 ___, Concluded

7.

	Post-Closing Trial Balance		

PROBLEM 4-4 ___

1., 3., and 6.

GENERAL LEDGER

ACCOUNT *Cash*   ACCOUNT NO. *11*

DATE	ITEM	POST. REF.	DEBIT	CREDIT	BALANCE DEBIT	BALANCE CREDIT

ACCOUNT *Supplies*   ACCOUNT NO. *13*

DATE	ITEM	POST. REF.	DEBIT	CREDIT	BALANCE DEBIT	BALANCE CREDIT

ACCOUNT *Prepaid Insurance*   ACCOUNT NO. *14*

DATE	ITEM	POST. REF.	DEBIT	CREDIT	BALANCE DEBIT	BALANCE CREDIT

ACCOUNT *Equipment*   ACCOUNT NO. *16*

DATE	ITEM	POST. REF.	DEBIT	CREDIT	BALANCE DEBIT	BALANCE CREDIT

ACCOUNT *Accumulated Depreciation—Equipment*   ACCOUNT NO. *17*

DATE	ITEM	POST. REF.	DEBIT	CREDIT	BALANCE DEBIT	BALANCE CREDIT

PROBLEM 4-4 ___ , Continued

ACCOUNT   *Trucks*   ACCOUNT NO.   *18*

DATE		ITEM	POST. REF.	DEBIT	CREDIT	BALANCE	
						DEBIT	CREDIT

ACCOUNT   *Accumulated Depreciation—Trucks*   ACCOUNT NO.   *19*

DATE		ITEM	POST. REF.	DEBIT	CREDIT	BALANCE	
						DEBIT	CREDIT

ACCOUNT   *Accounts Payable*   ACCOUNT NO.   *21*

DATE		ITEM	POST. REF.	DEBIT	CREDIT	BALANCE	
						DEBIT	CREDIT

ACCOUNT   *Wages Payable*   ACCOUNT NO.   *22*

DATE		ITEM	POST. REF.	DEBIT	CREDIT	BALANCE	
						DEBIT	CREDIT

ACCOUNT   *Common Stock*   ACCOUNT NO.   *31*

DATE		ITEM	POST. REF.	DEBIT	CREDIT	BALANCE	
						DEBIT	CREDIT

PROBLEM 4-4 ___ , Continued

ACCOUNT   *Retained Earnings*   ACCOUNT NO. *32*

DATE		ITEM	POST. REF.	DEBIT	CREDIT	BALANCE	
						DEBIT	CREDIT

ACCOUNT   *Dividends*   ACCOUNT NO. *33*

DATE		ITEM	POST. REF.	DEBIT	CREDIT	BALANCE	
						DEBIT	CREDIT

ACCOUNT   *Income Summary*   ACCOUNT NO. *34*

DATE		ITEM	POST. REF.	DEBIT	CREDIT	BALANCE	
						DEBIT	CREDIT

ACCOUNT   *Service Revenue*   ACCOUNT NO. *41*

DATE		ITEM	POST. REF.	DEBIT	CREDIT	BALANCE	
						DEBIT	CREDIT

PROBLEM 4-4 ___ , Continued

ACCOUNT   *Wages Expense*   ACCOUNT NO. 51

DATE		ITEM	POST. REF.	DEBIT	CREDIT	BALANCE	
						DEBIT	CREDIT

ACCOUNT   *Supplies Expense*   ACCOUNT NO.

DATE		ITEM	POST. REF.	DEBIT	CREDIT	BALANCE	
						DEBIT	CREDIT

ACCOUNT   *Rent Expense*   ACCOUNT NO.

DATE		ITEM	POST. REF.	DEBIT	CREDIT	BALANCE	
						DEBIT	CREDIT

ACCOUNT   *Depreciation Expense—Equipment*   ACCOUNT NO.

DATE		ITEM	POST. REF.	DEBIT	CREDIT	BALANCE	
						DEBIT	CREDIT

ACCOUNT   *Truck Expense*   ACCOUNT NO.

DATE		ITEM	POST. REF.	DEBIT	CREDIT	BALANCE	
						DEBIT	CREDIT

PROBLEM 4-4 ___, Continued

ACCOUNT *Depreciation Expense—Trucks*   ACCOUNT NO. 56

DATE	ITEM	POST. REF.	DEBIT	CREDIT	BALANCE DEBIT	BALANCE CREDIT

ACCOUNT *Insurance Expense*   ACCOUNT NO. 57

DATE	ITEM	POST. REF.	DEBIT	CREDIT	BALANCE DEBIT	BALANCE CREDIT

ACCOUNT *Miscellaneous Expense*   ACCOUNT NO. 59

DATE	ITEM	POST. REF.	DEBIT	CREDIT	BALANCE DEBIT	BALANCE CREDIT

174

PROBLEM 4-4 ____, Continued

2. Optional (Appendix)

End-of-Period Spreadsheet (Work Sheet)

	A	B	C	D	E	F	G	H	I	J	K
	Account Title	Unadjusted Trial Balance		Adjustments		Adjusted Trial Balance		Income Statement		Balance Sheet	
		Dr.	Cr.	Dr.	Cr.	Dr.	Cr.	Dr.	Cr.	Dr.	Cr.
1											
2											
3											
4											
5											
6											
7											
8											
9											
10											
11											
12											
13											
14											
15											
16											
17											
18											
19											
20											
21											
22											
23											
24											
25											
26											
27											
28											
29											
30											
31											
32											

PROBLEM 4-4 ___ , Continued

3.

JOURNAL   PAGE 26

	DATE		DESCRIPTION	POST. REF.	DEBIT	CREDIT	
1			*Adjusting Entries*				1
2							2
3							3
4							4
5							5
6							6
7							7
8							8
9							9
10							10
11							11
12							12
13							13
14							14
15							15
16							16
17							17
18							18
19							19
20							20
21							21
22							22
23							23
24							24
25							25
26							26
27							27
28							28
29							29
30							30
31							31
32							32
33							33
34							34
35							35

PROBLEM 4-4 ___, Continued

4.

	Adjusted Trial Balance		

PROBLEM 4-4 ___, Continued

5.

	Income Statement		

	Retained Earnings Statement		

PROBLEM 4-4 ___ , Continued

	Balance Sheet			

PROBLEM 4-4 ___ , Continued

6.

	JOURNAL				PAGE 27

	DATE		DESCRIPTION	POST. REF.	DEBIT	CREDIT	
1			*Closing Entries*				1
2							2
3							3
4							4
5							5
6							6
7							7
8							8
9							9
10							10
11							11
12							12
13							13
14							14
15							15
16							16
17							17
18							18
19							19
20							20
21							21
22							22
23							23
24							24
25							25
26							26
27							27
28							28
29							29
30							30
31							31
32							32
33							33
34							34
35							35

PROBLEM 4-4 ___ , Concluded

7.

Post-Closing Trial Balance			

PROBLEM 4-5 ___

1. and 2.

JOURNAL

PAGE *1*

	DATE		DESCRIPTION	POST. REF.	DEBIT	CREDIT	
1							1
2							2
3							3
4							4
5							5
6							6
7							7
8							8
9							9
10							10
11							11
12							12
13							13
14							14
15							15
16							16
17							17
18							18
19							19
20							20
21							21
22							22
23							23
24							24
25							25
26							26
27							27
28							28
29							29
30							30
31							31
32							32
33							33
34							34
35							35

PROBLEM 4-5 ___, Continued

JOURNAL   PAGE 2

	DATE		DESCRIPTION	POST. REF.	DEBIT	CREDIT	
1							1
2							2
3							3
4							4
5							5
6							6
7							7
8							8
9							9
10							10
11							11
12							12
13							13
14							14
15							15
16							16
17							17
18							18
19							19
20							20
21							21
22							22
23							23
24							24
25							25
26							26
27							27
28							28
29							29
30							30
31							31
32							32
33							33
34							34
35							35
36							36

PROBLEM 4-5 ___, Continued

2., 6., and 9.

GENERAL LEDGER

ACCOUNT   *Cash*   ACCOUNT NO.   *11*

DATE		ITEM	POST. REF.	DEBIT	CREDIT	BALANCE	
						DEBIT	CREDIT

ACCOUNT   *Accounts Receivable*   ACCOUNT NO.   *12*

DATE		ITEM	POST. REF.	DEBIT	CREDIT	BALANCE	
						DEBIT	CREDIT

PROBLEM 4-5 ___, Continued

ACCOUNT *Supplies* ACCOUNT NO. **14**

DATE		ITEM	POST. REF.	DEBIT	CREDIT	BALANCE	
						DEBIT	CREDIT

ACCOUNT *Prepaid Rent* ACCOUNT NO. **15**

DATE		ITEM	POST. REF.	DEBIT	CREDIT	BALANCE	
						DEBIT	CREDIT

ACCOUNT *Prepaid Insurance* ACCOUNT NO. **16**

DATE		ITEM	POST. REF.	DEBIT	CREDIT	BALANCE	
						DEBIT	CREDIT

ACCOUNT *Office Equipment* ACCOUNT NO. **18**

DATE		ITEM	POST. REF.	DEBIT	CREDIT	BALANCE	
						DEBIT	CREDIT

ACCOUNT *Accumulated Depreciation* ACCOUNT NO. **19**

DATE		ITEM	POST. REF.	DEBIT	CREDIT	BALANCE	
						DEBIT	CREDIT

PROBLEM 4-5 ___, Continued

ACCOUNT *Accounts Payable*   ACCOUNT NO. 21

DATE		ITEM	POST. REF.	DEBIT	CREDIT	BALANCE	
						DEBIT	CREDIT

ACCOUNT *Salaries Payable*   ACCOUNT NO. 22

DATE		ITEM	POST. REF.	DEBIT	CREDIT	BALANCE	
						DEBIT	CREDIT

ACCOUNT *Unearned Fees*   ACCOUNT NO. 23

DATE		ITEM	POST. REF.	DEBIT	CREDIT	BALANCE	
						DEBIT	CREDIT

ACCOUNT *Common Stock*   ACCOUNT NO. 31

DATE		ITEM	POST. REF.	DEBIT	CREDIT	BALANCE	
						DEBIT	CREDIT

ACCOUNT *Retained Earnings*   ACCOUNT NO. 32

DATE		ITEM	POST. REF.	DEBIT	CREDIT	BALANCE	
						DEBIT	CREDIT

PROBLEM 4-5 ____, Continued

ACCOUNT   *Dividends*   ACCOUNT NO. *33*

DATE	ITEM	POST. REF.	DEBIT	CREDIT	BALANCE DEBIT	BALANCE CREDIT

ACCOUNT   *Income Summary*   ACCOUNT NO. *34*

DATE	ITEM	POST. REF.	DEBIT	CREDIT	BALANCE DEBIT	BALANCE CREDIT

ACCOUNT   *Fees Earned*   ACCOUNT NO. *41*

DATE	ITEM	POST. REF.	DEBIT	CREDIT	BALANCE DEBIT	BALANCE CREDIT

ACCOUNT   *Salary Expense*   ACCOUNT NO. *51*

DATE	ITEM	POST. REF.	DEBIT	CREDIT	BALANCE DEBIT	BALANCE CREDIT

PROBLEM 4-5 ___, Continued

ACCOUNT   *Rent Expense*   ACCOUNT NO. _____

DATE	ITEM	POST. REF.	DEBIT	CREDIT	BALANCE DEBIT	BALANCE CREDIT

ACCOUNT   *Supplies Expense*   ACCOUNT NO. _____

DATE	ITEM	POST. REF.	DEBIT	CREDIT	BALANCE DEBIT	BALANCE CREDIT

ACCOUNT   *Depreciation Expense*   ACCOUNT NO. 54

DATE	ITEM	POST. REF.	DEBIT	CREDIT	BALANCE DEBIT	BALANCE CREDIT

ACCOUNT   *Insurance Expense*   ACCOUNT NO. 55

DATE	ITEM	POST. REF.	DEBIT	CREDIT	BALANCE DEBIT	BALANCE CREDIT

PROBLEM 4-5 ___, Continued

ACCOUNT   *Miscellaneous Expense*   ACCOUNT NO. 59

DATE		ITEM	POST. REF.	DEBIT	CREDIT	BALANCE	
						DEBIT	CREDIT

PROBLEM 4-5 ___, Continued

3.

	Unadjusted Trial Balance			

Name _____

PROBLEM 4-5 _____, Continued

5. Optional (Appendix)

End-of-Period Spreadsheet (Work Sheet)

	Unadjusted Trial Balance		Adjustments		Adjusted Trial Balance		Income Statement		Balance Sheet	
Account Title	Dr.	Cr.	Dr.	Cr.	Dr.	Cr.	Dr.	Cr.	Dr.	Cr.
1										
2										
3										
4										
5										
6										
7										
8										
9										
10										
11										
12										
13										
14										
15										
16										
17										
18										
19										
20										
21										
22										
23										
24										
25										
26										
27										
28										
29										
30										

PROBLEM 4-5 ___, Continued

6.

JOURNAL   PAGE *3*

	DATE		DESCRIPTION	POST. REF.	DEBIT	CREDIT	
1			*Adjusting Entries*				1
2							2
3							3
4							4
5							5
6							6
7							7
8							8
9							9
10							10
11							11
12							12
13							13
14							14
15							15
16							16
17							17
18							18
19							19
20							20
21							21
22							22
23							23
24							24
25							25
26							26
27							27
28							28
29							29
30							30
31							31
32							32
33							33
34							34
35							35

PROBLEM 4-5 ___ , Continued

7.

Adjusted Trial Balance			

PROBLEM 4-5 ___ , Continued

8.

Income Statement		

Retained Earnings Statement		

PROBLEM 4-5 ___ , Continued

	Balance Sheet			

PROBLEM 4-5 ___, Continued

9.

	DATE		DESCRIPTION	POST. REF.	DEBIT	CREDIT	
1			*Closing Entries*				1
2							2
3							3
4							4
5							5
6							6
7							7
8							8
9							9
10							10
11							11
12							12
13							13
14							14
15							15
16							16
17							17
18							18
19							19
20							20
21							21
22							22
23							23
24							24
25							25
26							26
27							27
28							28
29							29
30							30
31							31
32							32
33							33
34							34
35							35

JOURNAL   PAGE 4

PROBLEM 4-5 ___, Concluded

10.

	Post-Closing Trial Balance			

CONTINUING PROBLEM
1. Optional (Appendix)

End-of-Period Spreadsheet (Work Sheet)

	A	B	C	D	E	F	G	H	I	J	K
	Account Title	Unadjusted Trial Balance		Adjustments		Adjusted Trial Balance		Income Statement		Balance Sheet	
		Dr.	Cr.	Dr.	Cr.	Dr.	Cr.	Dr.	Cr.	Dr.	Cr.
1											
2											
3											
4											
5											
6											
7											
8											
9											
10											
11											
12											
13											
14											
15											
16											
17											
18											
19											
20											
21											
22											
23											
24											
25											
26											
27											
28											
29											
30											
31											
32											
33											
34											

CONTINUING PROBLEM, Continued

2.

Income Statement

Retained Earnings Statement

CONTINUING PROBLEM, Continued

Balance Sheet		

CONTINUING PROBLEM, Continued

3. Note: Use the general ledger accounts provided in Chapter 3, page 116–122.

JOURNAL PAGE *4*

	DATE		DESCRIPTION	POST. REF.	DEBIT	CREDIT	
1			*Closing Entries*				1
2							2
3							3
4							4
5							5
6							6
7							7
8							8
9							9
10							10
11							11
12							12
13							13
14							14
15							15
16							16
17							17
18							18
19							19
20							20
21							21
22							22
23							23
24							24
25							25
26							26
27							27
28							28
29							29
30							30
31							31
32							32
33							33
34							34

CONTINUING PROBLEM, Concluded

4.

	Post-Closing Trial Balance		

This Page Not Used.

COMPREHENSIVE PROBLEM 1

1. and 2.

JOURNAL   PAGE 5

	DATE		DESCRIPTION	POST. REF.	DEBIT	CREDIT	
1							1
2							2
3							3
4							4
5							5
6							6
7							7
8							8
9							9
10							10
11							11
12							12
13							13
14							14
15							15
16							16
17							17
18							18
19							19
20							20
21							21
22							22
23							23
24							24
25							25
26							26
27							27
28							28
29							29
30							30
31							31
32							32
33							33
34							34
35							35

COMPREHENSIVE PROBLEM 1, Continued

JOURNAL

	DATE	DESCRIPTION	POST. REF.	DEBIT	CREDIT	
1						1
2						2
3						3
4						4
5						5
6						6
7						7
8						8
9						9
10						10
11						11
12						12
13						13
14						14
15						15
16						16
17						17
18						18
19						19
20						20
21						21
22						22
23						23
24						24
25						25
26						26
27						27
28						28
29						29
30						30
31						31
32						32
33						33
34						34
35						35

COMPREHENSIVE PROBLEM 1, Continued

2., 6., and 9.

GENERAL LEDGER

ACCOUNT   *Cash*   ACCOUNT NO.   11

DATE	ITEM	POST. REF.	DEBIT	CREDIT	BALANCE DEBIT	BALANCE CREDIT

ACCOUNT   *Accounts Receivable*   ACCOUNT NO.   12

DATE	ITEM	POST. REF.	DEBIT	CREDIT	BALANCE DEBIT	BALANCE CREDIT

COMPREHENSIVE PROBLEM 1, Continued

ACCOUNT *Supplies* ACCOUNT NO. *14*

DATE		ITEM	POST. REF.	DEBIT	CREDIT	BALANCE	
						DEBIT	CREDIT

ACCOUNT *Prepaid Rent* ACCOUNT NO. *15*

DATE		ITEM	POST. REF.	DEBIT	CREDIT	BALANCE	
						DEBIT	CREDIT

ACCOUNT *Prepaid Insurance* ACCOUNT NO. *16*

DATE		ITEM	POST. REF.	DEBIT	CREDIT	BALANCE	
						DEBIT	CREDIT

ACCOUNT *Office Equipment* ACCOUNT NO. *18*

DATE		ITEM	POST. REF.	DEBIT	CREDIT	BALANCE	
						DEBIT	CREDIT

ACCOUNT *Accumulated Depreciation—Office Equipment* ACCOUNT NO. *19*

DATE		ITEM	POST. REF.	DEBIT	CREDIT	BALANCE	
						DEBIT	CREDIT

COMPREHENSIVE PROBLEM 1, Continued

ACCOUNT *Accounts Payable* ACCOUNT NO. 21

DATE		ITEM	POST. REF.	DEBIT	CREDIT	BALANCE DEBIT	CREDIT

ACCOUNT *Salaries Payable* ACCOUNT NO. 22

DATE		ITEM	POST. REF.	DEBIT	CREDIT	BALANCE DEBIT	CREDIT

ACCOUNT *Unearned Fees* ACCOUNT NO. 23

DATE		ITEM	POST. REF.	DEBIT	CREDIT	BALANCE DEBIT	CREDIT

ACCOUNT *Common Stock* ACCOUNT NO. 31

DATE		ITEM	POST. REF.	DEBIT	CREDIT	BALANCE DEBIT	CREDIT

COMPREHENSIVE PROBLEM 1, Continued

ACCOUNT *Retained Earnings*   ACCOUNT NO. 32

DATE		ITEM	POST. REF.	DEBIT	CREDIT	BALANCE	
						DEBIT	CREDIT

ACCOUNT *Dividends*   ACCOUNT NO. 33

DATE		ITEM	POST. REF.	DEBIT	CREDIT	BALANCE	
						DEBIT	CREDIT

ACCOUNT *Income Summary*   ACCOUNT NO. 34

DATE		ITEM	POST. REF.	DEBIT	CREDIT	BALANCE	
						DEBIT	CREDIT

ACCOUNT *Fees Earned*   ACCOUNT NO. 41

DATE		ITEM	POST. REF.	DEBIT	CREDIT	BALANCE	
						DEBIT	CREDIT

COMPREHENSIVE PROBLEM 1, Continued

ACCOUNT   *Salary Expense*   ACCOUNT NO. 51

DATE		ITEM	POST. REF.	DEBIT	CREDIT	BALANCE	
						DEBIT	CREDIT

ACCOUNT   *Rent Expense*   ACCOUNT NO. 52

DATE		ITEM	POST. REF.	DEBIT	CREDIT	BALANCE	
						DEBIT	CREDIT

ACCOUNT   *Supplies Expense*   ACCOUNT NO. 53

DATE		ITEM	POST. REF.	DEBIT	CREDIT	BALANCE	
						DEBIT	CREDIT

ACCOUNT   *Depreciation Expense—Office Equipment*   ACCOUNT NO. 54

DATE		ITEM	POST. REF.	DEBIT	CREDIT	BALANCE	
						DEBIT	CREDIT

COMPREHENSIVE PROBLEM 1, Continued

ACCOUNT   *Insurance Expense*   ACCOUNT NO. 55

DATE		ITEM	POST. REF.	DEBIT	CREDIT	BALANCE	
						DEBIT	CREDIT

ACCOUNT   *Miscellaneous Expense*   ACCOUNT NO. 59

DATE		ITEM	POST. REF.	DEBIT	CREDIT	BALANCE	
						DEBIT	CREDIT

COMPREHENSIVE PROBLEM 1, Continued

3.

	Unadjusted Trial Balance		

Name _____

COMPREHENSIVE PROBLEM 1, Continued

5. Optional (Appendix)

End-of-Period Spreadsheet (Work Sheet)

	A	B	C	D	E	F	G	H	I	J	K
	Account Title	Unadjusted Trial Balance		Adjustments		Adjusted Trial Balance		Income Statement		Balance Sheet	
		Dr.	Cr.	Dr.	Cr.	Dr.	Cr.	Dr.	Cr.	Dr.	Cr.
1											
2											
3											
4											
5											
6											
7											
8											
9											
10											
11											
12											
13											
14											
15											
16											
17											
18											
19											
20											
21											
22											
23											
24											
25											
26											
27											
28											
29											
30											

COMPREHENSIVE PROBLEM 1, Continued

6.

	JOURNAL				PAGE 7

	DATE		DESCRIPTION	POST. REF.	DEBIT	CREDIT	
1			*Adjusting Entries*				1
2							2
3							3
4							4
5							5
6							6
7							7
8							8
9							9
10							10
11							11
12							12
13							13
14							14
15							15
16							16
17							17
18							18
19							19
20							20
21							21
22							22
23							23
24							24
25							25
26							26
27							27
28							28
29							29
30							30
31							31
32							32
33							33
34							34

COMPREHENSIVE PROBLEM 1, Continued

7.

	Adjusted Trial Balance		

COMPREHENSIVE PROBLEM 1, Continued

8.

	Income Statement		

	Retained Earnings Statement		

COMPREHENSIVE PROBLEM 1, Continued

	Balance Sheet		

COMPREHENSIVE PROBLEM 1, Continued

9.

JOURNAL

	DATE		DESCRIPTION	POST. REF.	DEBIT	CREDIT	
1			*Closing Entries*				1
2							2
3							3
4							4
5							5
6							6
7							7
8							8
9							9
10							10
11							11
12							12
13							13
14							14
15							15
16							16
17							17
18							18
19							19
20							20
21							21
22							22
23							23
24							24
25							25
26							26
27							27
28							28
29							29
30							30
31							31
32							32
33							33
34							34
35							35

COMPREHENSIVE PROBLEM 1, Concluded

10.

Post-Closing Trial Balance

EXERCISE 5-1

A. _____

B. _____

C. _____

_____

_____

_____

_____

_____

EXERCISE 5-2

_____

EXERCISE 5-3

A. _____

_____

_____

B. _____

EXERCISE 5-4

_____

_____

EXERCISE 5-5

A. _____

_____

_____

B. _____

_____

_____

C. _____

_____

_____

D. _____

_____

_____

EXERCISE 5-6

A., B., C., and D.

JOURNAL

PAGE

	DATE		DESCRIPTION	POST. REF.	DEBIT	CREDIT	
1							1
2							2
3							3
4							4
5							5
6							6
7							7
8							8
9							9
10							10
11							11
12							12
13							13
14							14
15							15

EXERCISE 5-7

JOURNAL   PAGE

	DATE		DESCRIPTION	POST. REF.	DEBIT	CREDIT	
1							1
2							2
3							3
4							4
5							5
6							6
7							7
8							8
9							9
10							10
11							11
12							12
13							13
14							14
15							15
16							16
17							17
18							18
19							19
20							20
21							21
22							22
23							23
24							24

EXERCISE 5-8

JOURNAL

PAGE

	DATE		DESCRIPTION	POST. REF.	DEBIT	CREDIT	
1							1
2							2
3							3
4							4
5							5
6							6
7							7
8							8
9							9
10							10
11							11
12							12
13							13
14							14
15							15
16							16
17							17
18							18
19							19
20							20
21							21
22							22
23							23
24							24
25							25
26							26
27							27
28							28
29							29
30							30
31							31
32							32
33							33
34							34
35							35
36							36

EXERCISE 5-9

A. and B.

JOURNAL   PAGE

	DATE		DESCRIPTION	POST. REF.	DEBIT	CREDIT	
1							1
2							2
3							3
4							4
5							5
6							6
7							7
8							8

EXERCISE 5-10

A., B., and C.

JOURNAL

PAGE _____

	DATE		DESCRIPTION	POST. REF.	DEBIT	CREDIT	
1							1
2							2
3							3
4							4
5							5
6							6
7							7
8							8
9							9
10							10
11							11
12							12
13							13
14							14
15							15
16							16
17							17
18							18
19							19
20							20
21							21
22							22
23							23
24							24

EXERCISE 5-11

A. _____

B.

JOURNAL   PAGE

	DATE		DESCRIPTION	POST. REF.	DEBIT	CREDIT	
1							1
2							2
3							3
4							4
5							5
6							6
7							7
8							8

EXERCISE 5-12

A. _____
_____
_____

B. _____
_____
_____

C. _____
_____
_____

D. _____
_____
_____

E. _____
_____
_____

EXERCISE 5-13

A., B., and C.

JOURNAL   PAGE

	DATE		DESCRIPTION	POST. REF.	DEBIT	CREDIT	
1							1
2							2
3							3
4							4
5							5
6							6
7							7
8							8
9							9
10							10
11							11
12							12
13							13
14							14
15							15

EXERCISE 5-14

	Merchandise	Freight Paid by Seller		Customer Returns and Allowances	Amount to be Paid in Full
A.	$32,000	—	FOB destination, n/30	$1,600	$_____
B.	12,800	$300	FOB shipping point, 2/10, n/30	2,500	$_____
C.	21,000	—	FOB shipping point, 1/10, n/30	4,000	$_____
D.	9,000	175	FOB shipping point, 2/10, n/30	1,000	$_____
E.	77,400	—	FOB destination, 1/10, n/30	—	$_____

EXERCISE 5-15

A., B., and C.

	JOURNAL				PAGE

	DATE		DESCRIPTION	POST. REF.	DEBIT	CREDIT	
1							1
2							2
3							3
4							4
5							5
6							6
7							7
8							8
9							9
10							10
11							11
12							12
13							13
14							14
15							15
16							16
17							17
18							18
19							19
20							20
21							21
22							22
23							23
24							24

EXERCISE 5-16

A., B., and C.

JOURNAL

PAGE

	DATE		DESCRIPTION	POST. REF.	DEBIT	CREDIT	
1							1
2							2
3							3
4							4
5							5
6							6
7							7
8							8
9							9
10							10
11							11
12							12
13							13
14							14

EXERCISE 5-17

Balance Sheet Accounts		Income Statement Accounts	
Acct. #	Account Name	Acct. #	Account Name

EXERCISE 5-18

A. _____

B. _____

C. _____

D. _____

EXERCISE 5-19

JOURNAL   PAGE

	DATE		DESCRIPTION	POST. REF.	DEBIT	CREDIT	
1							1
2							2
3							3
4							4
5							5
6							6
7							7
8							8
9							9
10							10
11							11
12							12

EXERCISE 5-20

		Debit	Credit
A.	Cost of Goods Sold	_____	_____
B.	Customer Refunds Payable	_____	_____
C.	Delivery Expense	_____	_____
D.	Estimated Returns Inventory	_____	_____
E.	Inventory	_____	_____
F.	Sales	_____	_____
G.	Sales Tax Payable	_____	_____

EXERCISE 5-21

A. Gross profit: _____

B. _____

_____

C. _____

_____

D. _____

_____

EXERCISE 5-22

1. Advertising expense: _____

2. Depreciation expense on store equipment: _____

3. Insurance expense on office equipment: _____

4. Interest expense on notes payable: _____

5. Rent expense on office building: _____

6. Salaries of office personnel: _____

7. Salary of sales manager: _____

8. Sales supplies used: _____

EXERCISE 5-23

Sales	$735,000	B. $_____		$8,220,000	D. $_____		
Cost of goods sold	A. _____		157,850	C. _____		44,500	
Gross profit	110,000		42,150	2,300,000		15,500	

EXERCISE 5-24

A.

	Income Statement			

B. _____

_____

_____

_____

_____

_____

_____

EXERCISE 5-25

A. _____

_____

_____

_____

_____

_____

_____

_____

_____

_____

_____

_____

_____

_____

_____

_____

_____

_____

B.

	Income Statement			

EXERCISE 5-26

Income Statement

EXERCISE 5-27

JOURNAL   PAGE _____

	DATE		DESCRIPTION	POST. REF.	DEBIT	CREDIT	
1							1
2							2
3							3
4							4
5							5
6							6
7							7
8							8
9							9
10							10

EXERCISE 5-28

A. and B.

JOURNAL   PAGE

	DATE		DESCRIPTION	POST. REF.	DEBIT	CREDIT	
1							1
2							2
3							3
4							4
5							5
6							6
7							7
8							8
9							9
10							10
11							11
12							12
13							13
14							14
15							15
16							16
17							17
18							18

EXERCISE 5-29

JOURNAL   PAGE

	DATE		DESCRIPTION	POST. REF.	DEBIT	CREDIT	
1							1
2							2
3							3
4							4
5							5

EXERCISE 5-30

A. Accounts Payable: _____

B. Advertising Expense: _____

C. Cost of Goods Sold: _____

D. Dividends: _____

E. Inventory: _____

F. Sales: _____

G. Supplies: _____

H. Supplies Expense: _____

I. Wages Payable: _____

EXERCISE 5-31

JOURNAL   PAGE

	DATE		DESCRIPTION	POST. REF.	DEBIT	CREDIT	
1			*Closing Entries*				1
2							2
3							3
4							4
5							5
6							6
7							7
8							8
9							9
10							10
11							11
12							12
13							13
14							14
15							15
16							16
17							17
18							18
19							19
20							20
21							21
22							22
23							23
24							24

EXERCISE 5-32

JOURNAL   PAGE

	DATE		DESCRIPTION	POST. REF.	DEBIT	CREDIT	
1			*Closing Entries*				1
2							2
3							3
4							4
5							5
6							6
7							7
8							8
9							9
10							10
11							11
12							12
13							13
14							14
15							15
16							16
17							17
18							18
19							19
20							20
21							21
22							22
23							23
24							24

APPENDIX EXERCISE 5-33

Account	Increase	Decrease	Normal Balance
Purchases	debit	A. _____	B. _____
Purchase Discounts	credit	C. _____	credit
Purchase Returns and Allowances	D. _____	E. _____	F. _____
Freight In	debit	G. _____	debit

APPENDIX EXERCISE 5-34

JOURNAL

	DATE	DESCRIPTION	POST. REF.	DEBIT	CREDIT	
1						1
2						2
3						3
4						4
5						5
6						6
7						7
8						8
9						9
10						10
11						11
12						12
13						13
14						14
15						15
16						16
17						17
18						18
19						19
20						20
21						21
22						22
23						23
24						24
25						25
26						26
27						27
28						28

APPENDIX EXERCISE 5-35

A. Purchases $-$ (X + Y) = Net purchases

_____

B. Net purchases + X = Cost of inventory purchased

_____

C. Inventory (beginning) + Cost of inventory purchased = X

_____

D. Inventory available for sale $-$ X = Cost of inventory before estimated returns

_____

E. Cost of goods sold before estimated returns $-$ X = Cost of goods sold

_____

APPENDIX EXERCISE 5-36

A.

B. _____

C. _____

_____

APPENDIX EXERCISE 5-37

APPENDIX EXERCISE 5-38

APPENDIX EXERCISE 5-39

_____

_____

_____

_____

_____

_____

_____

_____

_____

_____

_____

_____

_____

_____

_____

_____

_____

(Optional)

APPENDIX EXERCISE 5-40

JOURNAL
PAGE

	DATE		DESCRIPTION	POST. REF.	DEBIT	CREDIT	
1			*Closing Entries*				1
2							2
3							3
4							4
5							5
6							6
7							7
8							8
9							9
10							10
11							11
12							12
13							13
14							14
15							15
16							16
17							17
18							18
19							19
20							20
21							21
22							22
23							23
24							24
25							25
26							26
27							27
28							28

This Page Not Used.

PROBLEM 5-1 ___

JOURNAL

PAGE

	DATE		DESCRIPTION	POST. REF.	DEBIT	CREDIT	
1							1
2							2
3							3
4							4
5							5
6							6
7							7
8							8
9							9
10							10
11							11
12							12
13							13
14							14
15							15
16							16
17							17
18							18
19							19
20							20
21							21
22							22
23							23
24							24
25							25
26							26
27							27
28							28
29							29
30							30
31							31
32							32
33							33
34							34
35							35
36							36

PROBLEM 5-1 ___, Concluded

	DATE		DESCRIPTION	POST. REF.	DEBIT	CREDIT	
1							1
2							2
3							3
4							4
5							5
6							6
7							7
8							8
9							9
10							10
11							11
12							12
13							13
14							14
15							15
16							16
17							17
18							18
19							19
20							20
21							21
22							22
23							23
24							24
25							25
26							26
27							27
28							28
29							29
30							30
31							31
32							32
33							33
34							34
35							35
36							36

PROBLEM 5-2 ___

JOURNAL   PAGE

	DATE	DESCRIPTION	POST. REF.	DEBIT	CREDIT	
1						1
2						2
3						3
4						4
5						5
6						6
7						7
8						8
9						9
10						10
11						11
12						12
13						13
14						14
15						15
16						16
17						17
18						18
19						19
20						20
21						21
22						22
23						23
24						24
25						25
26						26
27						27
28						28
29						29
30						30
31						31
32						32
33						33
34						34
35						35
36						36

PROBLEM 5-2 ___, Continued

JOURNAL

	DATE		DESCRIPTION	POST. REF.	DEBIT	CREDIT	
1							1
2							2
3							3
4							4
5							5
6							6
7							7
8							8
9							9
10							10
11							11
12							12
13							13
14							14
15							15
16							16
17							17
18							18
19							19
20							20
21							21
22							22
23							23
24							24
25							25
26							26
27							27
28							28
29							29
30							30
31							31
32							32
33							33
34							34
35							35
36							36

PROBLEM 5-2 ___, Concluded

JOURNAL

PAGE

	DATE		DESCRIPTION	POST. REF.	DEBIT	CREDIT	
1							1
2							2
3							3
4							4
5							5
6							6
7							7
8							8
9							9
10							10
11							11
12							12
13							13
14							14
15							15
16							16
17							17
18							18
19							19
20							20
21							21
22							22
23							23
24							24
25							25
26							26
27							27
28							28
29							29
30							30
31							31
32							32
33							33
34							34
35							35
36							36

This Page Not Used.

PROBLEM 5-3 ___

JOURNAL

	DATE		DESCRIPTION	POST. REF.	DEBIT	CREDIT	
1							1
2							2
3							3
4							4
5							5
6							6
7							7
8							8
9							9
10							10
11							11
12							12
13							13
14							14
15							15
16							16
17							17
18							18
19							19
20							20
21							21
22							22
23							23
24							24
25							25
26							26
27							27
28							28
29							29
30							30
31							31
32							32
33							33
34							34
35							35
36							36

PROBLEM 5-3 ___, Concluded

JOURNAL

	DATE		DESCRIPTION	POST. REF.	DEBIT	CREDIT	
1							1
2							2
3							3
4							4
5							5
6							6
7							7
8							8
9							9
10							10
11							11
12							12
13							13
14							14
15							15
16							16
17							17
18							18
19							19
20							20
21							21
22							22
23							23
24							24
25							25
26							26
27							27
28							28
29							29
30							30
31							31
32							32
33							33
34							34
35							35
36							36

PROBLEM 5-4 ___

1.

					JOURNAL							PAGE	

	DATE		DESCRIPTION	POST. REF.	DEBIT	CREDIT	
1							1
2							2
3							3
4							4
5							5
6							6
7							7
8							8
9							9
10							10
11							11
12							12
13							13
14							14
15							15
16							16
17							17
18							18
19							19
20							20
21							21
22							22
23							23
24							24
25							25
26							26
27							27
28							28
29							29
30							30
31							31
32							32
33							33
34							34
35							35

PROBLEM 5-4 ___, Continued

JOURNAL   PAGE

	DATE		DESCRIPTION	POST. REF.	DEBIT	CREDIT	
1							1
2							2
3							3
4							4
5							5
6							6
7							7
8							8
9							9
10							10
11							11
12							12
13							13
14							14
15							15
16							16
17							17
18							18
19							19
20							20
21							21
22							22
23							23
24							24
25							25
26							26
27							27
28							28
29							29
30							30
31							31
32							32
33							33
34							34
35							35
36							36

PROBLEM 5-4 ___ , Concluded

2.

	DATE		DESCRIPTION	POST. REF.	DEBIT	CREDIT	
1							1
2							2
3							3
4							4
5							5
6							6
7							7
8							8
9							9
10							10
11							11
12							12
13							13
14							14
15							15
16							16
17							17
18							18
19							19
20							20
21							21
22							22
23							23
24							24
25							25
26							26
27							27
28							28
29							29
30							30
31							31
32							32
33							33
34							34
35							35

JOURNAL — PAGE

This Page Not Used.

PROBLEM 5-5 ___

1.

	Income Statement		

PROBLEM 5-5 ___, Continued

2.

Retained Earnings Statement

PROBLEM 5-5 ___, Continued

3.

	Balance Sheet		

PROBLEM 5-5 ___, Concluded

Balance Sheet (continued)

4. _____

_____

_____

_____

_____

_____

_____

PROBLEM 5-6 ___

1.

	Income Statement		

2.

	Retained Earnings Statement		

PROBLEM 5-6 ___, Continued

3.

	Balance Sheet		

PROBLEM 5-6 ___, Continued

Balance Sheet (continued)

PROBLEM 5-6 ___, Concluded

4.

JOURNAL   PAGE

	DATE		DESCRIPTION	POST. REF.	DEBIT	CREDIT	
1			*Closing Entries*				1
2							2
3							3
4							4
5							5
6							6
7							7
8							8
9							9
10							10
11							11
12							12
13							13
14							14
15							15
16							16
17							17
18							18
19							19
20							20
21							21
22							22
23							23
24							24
25							25
26							26
27							27
28							28
29							29
30							30
31							31
32							32
33							33
34							34
35							35

APPENDIX PROBLEM 5-7 ___

JOURNAL

	DATE	DESCRIPTION	POST. REF.	DEBIT	CREDIT	
1						1
2						2
3						3
4						4
5						5
6						6
7						7
8						8
9						9
10						10
11						11
12						12
13						13
14						14
15						15
16						16
17						17
18						18
19						19
20						20
21						21
22						22
23						23
24						24
25						25
26						26
27						27
28						28
29						29
30						30
31						31
32						32
33						33
34						34
35						35
36						36

APPENDIX PROBLEM 5-7 ___, Concluded

JOURNAL   PAGE

	DATE		DESCRIPTION	POST. REF.	DEBIT	CREDIT	
1							1
2							2
3							3
4							4
5							5
6							6
7							7
8							8
9							9
10							10
11							11
12							12
13							13
14							14
15							15
16							16
17							17
18							18
19							19
20							20
21							21
22							22
23							23
24							24
25							25
26							26
27							27
28							28
29							29
30							30
31							31
32							32
33							33
34							34
35							35
36							36

APPENDIX PROBLEM 5-8 ___

JOURNAL

	DATE	DESCRIPTION	POST. REF.	DEBIT	CREDIT	
1						1
2						2
3						3
4						4
5						5
6						6
7						7
8						8
9						9
10						10
11						11
12						12
13						13
14						14
15						15
16						16
17						17
18						18
19						19
20						20
21						21
22						22
23						23
24						24
25						25
26						26
27						27
28						28
29						29
30						30
31						31
32						32
33						33
34						34
35						35
36						36

APPENDIX PROBLEM 5-8 ___, Concluded

JOURNAL

	DATE		DESCRIPTION	POST. REF.	DEBIT	CREDIT	
1							1
2							2
3							3
4							4
5							5
6							6
7							7
8							8
9							9
10							10
11							11
12							12
13							13
14							14
15							15
16							16
17							17
18							18
19							19
20							20
21							21
22							22
23							23
24							24
25							25
26							26
27							27
28							28
29							29
30							30
31							31
32							32
33							33
34							34
35							35
36							36

APPENDIX PROBLEM 5-9 ___

1.

JOURNAL

PAGE

	DATE		DESCRIPTION	POST. REF.	DEBIT	CREDIT	
1							1
2							2
3							3
4							4
5							5
6							6
7							7
8							8
9							9
10							10
11							11
12							12
13							13
14							14
15							15
16							16
17							17
18							18
19							19
20							20
21							21
22							22
23							23
24							24
25							25
26							26
27							27
28							28
29							29
30							30
31							31
32							32
33							33
34							34
35							35

APPENDIX PROBLEM 5-9 ___, Concluded

2.

JOURNAL   PAGE

	DATE		DESCRIPTION	POST. REF.	DEBIT	CREDIT	
1							1
2							2
3							3
4							4
5							5
6							6
7							7
8							8
9							9
10							10
11							11
12							12
13							13
14							14
15							15
16							16
17							17
18							18
19							19
20							20
21							21
22							22
23							23
24							24
25							25
26							26
27							27
28							28
29							29
30							30
31							31
32							32
33							33
34							34
35							35

APPENDIX PROBLEM 5-10 ___

1. _____

_____

_____

_____

_____

2.

Income Statement			

APPENDIX PROBLEM 5-10 ___, Continued

Income Statement (continued)

APPENDIX PROBLEM 5-10 ___, Continued

3.

JOURNAL   PAGE

	DATE		DESCRIPTION	POST. REF.	DEBIT	CREDIT	
1			*Closing Entries*				1
2							2
3							3
4							4
5							5
6							6
7							7
8							8
9							9
10							10
11							11
12							12
13							13
14							14
15							15
16							16
17							17
18							18
19							19
20							20
21							21
22							22
23							23
24							24
25							25
26							26
27							27
28							28
29							29
30							30
31							31
32							32
33							33
34							34
35							35

APPENDIX PROBLEM 5-10 ___, Concluded

JOURNAL

PAGE

	DATE		DESCRIPTION	POST. REF.	DEBIT	CREDIT	
1			*Closing Entries*				1
2							2
3							3
4							4
5							5
6							6
7							7
8							8
9							9
10							10
11							11
12							12
13							13
14							14
15							15
16							16
17							17
18							18
19							19
20							20
21							21
22							22
23							23
24							24
25							25
26							26
27							27
28							28
29							29
30							30
31							31
32							32

4. _____

_____

COMPREHENSIVE PROBLEM 2

1., 2., 6., and 9.

GENERAL LEDGER

ACCOUNT _Cash_   ACCOUNT NO. _110_

DATE	ITEM	POST. REF.	DEBIT	CREDIT	BALANCE DEBIT	BALANCE CREDIT

ACCOUNT _Accounts Receivable_   ACCOUNT NO. _112_

DATE	ITEM	POST. REF.	DEBIT	CREDIT	BALANCE DEBIT	BALANCE CREDIT

COMPREHENSIVE PROBLEM 2, Continued

ACCOUNT *Inventory* ACCOUNT NO. **115**

DATE		ITEM	POST. REF.	DEBIT	CREDIT	BALANCE	
						DEBIT	CREDIT

ACCOUNT *Estimated Returns Inventory* ACCOUNT NO. **116**

DATE		ITEM	POST. REF.	DEBIT	CREDIT	BALANCE	
						DEBIT	CREDIT

ACCOUNT *Prepaid Insurance* ACCOUNT NO. **117**

DATE		ITEM	POST. REF.	DEBIT	CREDIT	BALANCE	
						DEBIT	CREDIT

COMPREHENSIVE PROBLEM 2, Continued

ACCOUNT   *Store Supplies*   ACCOUNT NO. 118

DATE		ITEM	POST. REF.	DEBIT	CREDIT	BALANCE	
						DEBIT	CREDIT

ACCOUNT   *Store Equipment*   ACCOUNT NO. 123

DATE		ITEM	POST. REF.	DEBIT	CREDIT	BALANCE	
						DEBIT	CREDIT

ACCOUNT   *Accumulated Depreciation—Store Equipment*   ACCOUNT NO. 124

DATE		ITEM	POST. REF.	DEBIT	CREDIT	BALANCE	
						DEBIT	CREDIT

ACCOUNT   *Accounts Payable*   ACCOUNT NO. 210

DATE		ITEM	POST. REF.	DEBIT	CREDIT	BALANCE	
						DEBIT	CREDIT

COMPREHENSIVE PROBLEM 2, Continued

ACCOUNT   *Salaries Payable*   ACCOUNT NO. *211*

DATE		ITEM	POST. REF.	DEBIT	CREDIT	BALANCE	
						DEBIT	CREDIT

ACCOUNT   *Customer Refunds Payable*   ACCOUNT NO. *212*

DATE		ITEM	POST. REF.	DEBIT	CREDIT	BALANCE	
						DEBIT	CREDIT

ACCOUNT   *Common Stock*   ACCOUNT NO. *310*

DATE		ITEM	POST. REF.	DEBIT	CREDIT	BALANCE	
						DEBIT	CREDIT

ACCOUNT   *Retained Earnings*   ACCOUNT NO. *311*

DATE		ITEM	POST. REF.	DEBIT	CREDIT	BALANCE	
						DEBIT	CREDIT

COMPREHENSIVE PROBLEM 2, Continued

ACCOUNT *Dividends*   ACCOUNT NO. *312*

DATE	ITEM	POST. REF.	DEBIT	CREDIT	BALANCE DEBIT	BALANCE CREDIT

ACCOUNT *Income Summary*   ACCOUNT NO. *313*

DATE	ITEM	POST. REF.	DEBIT	CREDIT	BALANCE DEBIT	BALANCE CREDIT

ACCOUNT *Sales*   ACCOUNT NO. *410*

DATE	ITEM	POST. REF.	DEBIT	CREDIT	BALANCE DEBIT	BALANCE CREDIT

COMPREHENSIVE PROBLEM 2, Continued

ACCOUNT   *Cost of Goods Sold*   ACCOUNT NO. 510

DATE	ITEM	POST. REF.	DEBIT	CREDIT	BALANCE DEBIT	BALANCE CREDIT

ACCOUNT   *Sales Salaries Expense*   ACCOUNT NO. 520

DATE	ITEM	POST. REF.	DEBIT	CREDIT	BALANCE DEBIT	BALANCE CREDIT

ACCOUNT   *Advertising Expense*   ACCOUNT NO. 521

DATE	ITEM	POST. REF.	DEBIT	CREDIT	BALANCE DEBIT	BALANCE CREDIT

ACCOUNT   *Depreciation Expense*   ACCOUNT NO. 522

DATE	ITEM	POST. REF.	DEBIT	CREDIT	BALANCE DEBIT	BALANCE CREDIT

COMPREHENSIVE PROBLEM 2, Continued

ACCOUNT   *Store Supplies Expense*   ACCOUNT NO.   *523*

DATE	ITEM	POST. REF.	DEBIT	CREDIT	BALANCE DEBIT	BALANCE CREDIT

ACCOUNT   *Miscellaneous Selling Expense*   ACCOUNT NO.   *529*

DATE	ITEM	POST. REF.	DEBIT	CREDIT	BALANCE DEBIT	BALANCE CREDIT

ACCOUNT   *Office Salaries Expense*   ACCOUNT NO.   *530*

DATE	ITEM	POST. REF.	DEBIT	CREDIT	BALANCE DEBIT	BALANCE CREDIT

ACCOUNT   *Rent Expense*   ACCOUNT NO.   *531*

DATE	ITEM	POST. REF.	DEBIT	CREDIT	BALANCE DEBIT	BALANCE CREDIT

COMPREHENSIVE PROBLEM 2, Continued

ACCOUNT   *Insurance Expense*   ACCOUNT NO. *532*

DATE		ITEM	POST. REF.	DEBIT	CREDIT	BALANCE	
						DEBIT	CREDIT

ACCOUNT   *Miscellaneous Administrative Expense*   ACCOUNT NO. *'0*

DATE		ITEM	POST. REF.	DEBIT	CREDIT	BALANCE	
						DEBIT	CREDIT

COMPREHENSIVE PROBLEM 2, Continued

1. and 2.

JOURNAL

	DATE		DESCRIPTION	POST. REF.	DEBIT	CREDIT	
1							1
2							2
3							3
4							4
5							5
6							6
7							7
8							8
9							9
10							10
11							11
12							12
13							13
14							14
15							15
16							16
17							17
18							18
19							19
20							20
21							21
22							22
23							23
24							24
25							25
26							26
27							27
28							28
29							29
30							30
31							31
32							32
33							33
34							34
35							35

COMPREHENSIVE PROBLEM 2, Continued

JOURNAL

PAGE 20
continued

	DATE		DESCRIPTION	POST. REF.	DEBIT	CREDIT	
1							1
2							2
3							3
4							4
5							5
6							6
7							7
8							8
9							9
10							10
11							11
12							12
13							13
14							14
15							15
16							16
17							17
18							18
19							19
20							20
21							21
22							22
23							23
24							24
25							25
26							26
27							27
28							28
29							29
30							30
31							31
32							32
33							33
34							34
35							35

COMPREHENSIVE PROBLEM 2, Continued

JOURNAL

	DATE		DESCRIPTION	POST. REF.	DEBIT	CREDIT	
1							1
2							2
3							3
4							4
5							5
6							6
7							7
8							8
9							9
10							10
11							11
12							12
13							13
14							14
15							15
16							16
17							17
18							18
19							19
20							20
21							21
22							22
23							23
24							24
25							25
26							26
27							27
28							28
29							29
30							30
31							31
32							32
33							33
34							34
35							35

COMPREHENSIVE PROBLEM 2, Continued

JOURNAL

PAGE *21*
continued

	DATE		DESCRIPTION	POST. REF.	DEBIT	CREDIT	
1							1
2							2
3							3
4							4
5							5
6							6
7							7
8							8
9							9
10							10
11							11
12							12
13							13
14							14
15							15
16							16
17							17
18							18
19							19
20							20
21							21
22							22
23							23
24							24
25							25
26							26
27							27
28							28
29							29
30							30
31							31
32							32
33							33
34							34
35							35

COMPREHENSIVE PROBLEM 2, Continued

3.

Unadjusted Trial Balance			

COMPREHENSIVE PROBLEM 2, Continued

4. and 6.

JOURNAL   PAGE 22

	DATE		DESCRIPTION	POST. REF.	DEBIT	CREDIT	
1			*Adjusting Entries*				1
2							2
3							3
4							4
5							5
6							6
7							7
8							8
9							9
10							10
11							11
12							12
13							13
14							14
15							15
16							16
17							17
18							18
19							19
20							20
21							21
22							22
23							23
24							24
25							25
26							26
27							27
28							28
29							29
30							30
31							31
32							32
33							33
34							34
35							35

COMPREHENSIVE PROBLEM 2, Continued

7.

Adjusted Trial Balance			

COMPREHENSIVE PROBLEM 2, Continued

8.

	Income Statement		

COMPREHENSIVE PROBLEM 2, Continued

Retained Earnings Statement		

COMPREHENSIVE PROBLEM 2, Continued

Balance Sheet		

COMPREHENSIVE PROBLEM 2, Continued

9.

JOURNAL

PAGE 23

	DATE		DESCRIPTION	POST. REF.	DEBIT	CREDIT	
1			*Closing Entries*				1
2							2
3							3
4							4
5							5
6							6
7							7
8							8
9							9
10							10
11							11
12							12
13							13
14							14
15							15
16							16
17							17
18							18
19							19
20							20
21							21
22							22
23							23
24							24
25							25
26							26
27							27
28							28
29							29
30							30
31							31
32							32
33							33
34							34
35							35

COMPREHENSIVE PROBLEM 2, Continued

10.

Post-Closing Trial Balance			

COMPREHENSIVE PROBLEM 2, Concluded

5. (Optional) *This work sheet is applicable only if the end-of-period spreadsheet (work sheet) is used.*

End-O-Period Spreadsheet (Work Sheet)

	A	B	C	D	E	F	G	H	I	J	K
	Account Title	Unadjusted Trial Balance		Adjustments		Adjusted Trial Balance		Income Statement		Balance Sheet	
		Dr.	Cr.	Dr.	Cr.	Dr.	Cr.	Dr.	Cr.	Dr.	Cr.
1											
2											
3											
4											
5											
6											
7											
8											
9											
10											
11											
12											
13											
14											
15											
16											
17											
18											
19											
20											
21											
22											
23											
24											
25											
26											
27											
28											
29											
30											
31											
32											
33											
34											

This Page Not Used.

EXERCISE 6-1

_____
_____
_____
_____
_____
_____
_____
_____
_____
_____
_____
_____
_____
_____
_____
_____
_____

EXERCISE 6-2

A. _____
_____
_____
_____
_____
_____

B. _____
_____
_____
_____
_____

C. _____
_____
_____
_____
_____

EXERCISE 6-3

A.

DVD Players

Date	Purchases			Cost of Goods Sold			Inventory		
	Quantity	Unit Cost	Total Cost	Quantity	Unit Cost	Total Cost	Quantity	Unit Cost	Total Cost

B.

_____
_____
_____

EXERCISE 6-4

DVD Players

Date	Purchases			Cost of Goods Sold			Inventory		
	Quantity	Unit Cost	Total Cost	Quantity	Unit Cost	Total Cost	Quantity	Unit Cost	Total Cost

EXERCISE 6-5

A.

Prepaid Cell Phones

Date	Purchases			Cost of Goods Sold			Inventory		
	Quantity	Unit Cost	Total Cost	Quantity	Unit Cost	Total Cost	Quantity	Unit Cost	Total Cost

B. _____

_____

EXERCISE 6-6

Prepaid Cell Phones

Date	Purchases			Cost of Goods Sold			Inventory		
	Quantity	Unit Cost	Total Cost	Quantity	Unit Cost	Total Cost	Quantity	Unit Cost	Total Cost

EXERCISE 6-7

A. FIFO: _____

B. LIFO: _____

EXERCISE 6-8

Date	Purchases			Cost of Goods Sold			Inventory		
	Quantity	Unit Cost	Total Cost	Quantity	Unit Cost	Total Cost	Quantity	Unit Cost	Total Cost

EXERCISE 6-9

Date	Purchases			Cost of Goods Sold			Inventory		
	Quantity	Unit Cost	Total Cost	Quantity	Unit Cost	Total Cost	Quantity	Unit Cost	Total Cost

Name _____

EXERCISE 6-10

Date	Purchases			Cost of Goods Sold			Inventory		
	Quantity	Unit Cost	Total Cost	Quantity	Unit Cost	Total Cost	Quantity	Unit Cost	Total Cost

EXERCISE 6-11

Date	Purchases			Cost of Goods Sold			Inventory		
	Quantity	Unit Cost	Total Cost	Quantity	Unit Cost	Total Cost	Quantity	Unit Cost	Total Cost

EXERCISE 6-12

A. First-in, first-out method: _____

_____

B. Last-in, first-out method: _____

_____

C. Weighted average cost method: _____

_____

_____

_____

_____

_____

_____

_____

EXERCISE 6-13

Inventory Method	Ending Inventory	Cost of Goods Sold
A. First-in, first-out............................	_____	_____
B. Last-in, first-out.............................	_____	_____
C. Weighted average cost....................	_____	_____

Supporting calculations:

_____

_____

_____

_____

_____

_____

_____

_____

_____

_____

_____

_____

_____

_____

_____

_____

_____

_____

_____

_____

_____

_____

_____

_____

_____

_____

_____

_____

_____

_____

_____

EXERCISE 6-14

A. 1. FIFO inventory _____ LIFO inventory

   2. FIFO cost of goods sold _____ LIFO cost of goods sold

   3. FIFO net income _____ LIFO net income

   4. FIFO income taxes _____ LIFO income taxes

B. _____

_____

_____

_____

_____

EXERCISE 6-15

	A	B	C	D	E	F	G
1				**Market Value per Unit (Net Realizable Value)**			
2							
3	**Product**	**Inventory Quantity**	**Cost per Unit**		**Cost**	**Market**	**LCM**
,	Model A	300	$140	$125			
.	Model B	500	90	112			
6	Model C	150	60	59			
7	Model D	800	120	115			
8	Model E	400	140	145			
9	Total						

EXERCISE 6-16

_____

_____

_____

_____

_____

_____

_____

EXERCISE 6-17

A.

20Y8 Balance Sheet

Inventory ....   _____

Current assets ....   _____

Total assets ....   _____

Stockholders' equity...................................   _____

B.

20Y8 Income

Statement

Cost of goods sold ....   _____

Gross profit ....   _____

Net income...   _____

C.

20Y9 Income

Statement

Cost of goods sold ....   _____

Gross profit ....   _____

Net income...   _____

D. _____

_____

_____

_____

EXERCISE 6-18

A.

                                              20Y1 Balance Sheet

Inventory ....   _____

Current assets..   _____

Total assets...   _____

Stockholders' equity...................................   _____

B.

                                              20Y1 Income

Statement

Cost of goods sold ....   _____

Gross profit ....   _____

Net income...   _____

C.

                                              20Y2 Income

Statement

Cost of goods sold ....   _____

Gross profit ....   _____

Net income...   _____

D. _____

_____

_____

_____

EXERCISE 6-19

_____

_____

_____

_____

_____

_____

_____

_____

_____

_____

_____

_____

_____

_____

_____

_____

APPENDIX EXERCISE 6-20

_____

APPENDIX EXERCISE 6-21

_____

APPENDIX EXERCISE 6-22

_____

APPENDIX EXERCISE 6-23

	A	B Cost	C Retail
1			
2			
3			
,			
.			
6			
7			
8			
9			
10			

APPENDIX EXERCISE 6-24

A.

	A	B	C
1			
2			
3			
,			
.			
6			
7			
8			
9			
10			

B. _____

_____

_____

_____

_____

APPENDIX EXERCISE 6-25

APPENDIX EXERCISE 6-26

PROBLEM 6-1 _____

1.

Date	Purchases			Cost of Goods Sold			Inventory		
	Quantity	Unit Cost	Total Cost	Quantity	Unit Cost	Total Cost	Quantity	Unit Cost	Total Cost

PROBLEM 6-1 ___, Concluded

2.

JOURNAL   ,!&%

	DATE		DESCRIPTION	POST. REF.	DEBIT	CREDIT	
.							.
/							/
0							0
1							1
2							2
3							3
4							4
5							5
6							6
.7							.7

3. _____

4. _____

5. _____

_____

_____

_____

_____

PROBLEM 6-2 ___

1.

Date	Purchases			Cost of Goods Sold			Inventory		
	Quantity	Unit Cost	Total Cost	Quantity	Unit Cost	Total Cost	Quantity	Unit Cost	Total Cost

Chapter 6

Name _____

PROBLEM 6-2____, Continued

Date	Purchases			Cost of Goods Sold			Inventory		
	Quantity	Unit Cost	Total Cost	Quantity	Unit Cost	Total Cost	Quantity	Unit Cost	Total Cost

PROBLEM 6-2 ___, Concluded

2.

3. _____

_____

This Page Not Used.

PROBLEM 6-3 _____

Date	Purchases			Cost of Goods Sold			Inventory		
	Quantity	Unit Cost	Total Cost	Quantity	Unit Cost	Total Cost	Quantity	Unit Cost	Total Cost

PROBLEM 6-3 ___, Concluded

2.

3. _____

_____

PROBLEM 6-4 ___

1., 2., and 3.

Inventory Method	Ending Inventory	Cost of Goods Sold
A. First-in, first-out...............................	_____	_____
B. Last-in, first-out...............................	_____	_____
C. Weighted average cost.....................	_____	_____

Supporting calculations:

_____

_____

_____

_____

_____

_____

_____

_____

_____

_____

_____

_____

_____

_____

_____

_____

_____

_____

_____

_____

_____

_____

_____

_____

_____

_____

_____

_____

_____

_____

_____

_____

PROBLEM 6-4 ___ , Concluded

_____

_____

_____

_____

_____

_____

_____

_____

_____

_____

_____

_____

_____

_____

_____

_____

_____

_____

_____

_____

_____

_____

_____

_____

_____

_____

_____

_____

_____

4.

	FIFO	LIFO	Weighted Average
Sales	_____	_____	_____
Cost of goods sold	_____	_____	_____
Gross profit	_____	_____	_____
Inventory, _____	_____	_____	_____

PROBLEM 6-5 ___

1.

First-In, First-Out Method

Model	Quantity	Unit Cost	Total Cost

2.

Last-In, First-Out Method

Model	Quantity	Unit Cost	Total Cost

PROBLEM 6-5 ___, Concluded

3.

Weighted Average Cost Method

Model	Quantity	Unit Cost	Total Cost

4. A. _____

_____

_____

_____

_____

_____

_____

_____

_____

_____

B. _____

_____

_____

_____

_____

PROBLEM 6-6 ___

	A	B	C	D	E	F	G
1	Inventory Sheet						
2	December 31						
3	Description	Inventory Quantity	Cost per Unit	Market Value per Unit (Net Realizable Value)	Cost	Market	LCM
6							
7							
8							
9							
10							
11							
12							
13							
14							
15							
16							
17							
18							
19							
20							
21							
22							
23							
24							
25							
26							
27							
28							
29							
30							
31							
32							
33							
34							
35							

This Page Not Used.

APPENDIX PROBLEM 6-7 ___

1.

	A	B	C
1			
2		**Cost**	**Retail**
3			
,			
.			
6			
7			
8			
9			
10			
11			
12			
13			
14			
15			
16			
17			
18			

2.

	A	B	C
1			
2			**Cost**
3	A.		
,			
.			
6			
7			
8			
9			
10			
11			
12			
13			
14			
15			
16			
17	B.		
18			
19			
20			
21			
22			
23			
24			

This Page Not Used.

EXERCISE 7-1

EXERCISE 7-1, Continued

EXERCISE 7-2

A. _____

_____

_____

_____

B. _____

_____

_____

_____

_____

_____

C. _____

_____

_____

_____

_____

_____

_____

_____

_____

_____

_____

EXERCISE 7-3

A. _____

_____

_____

B. _____

_____

_____

_____

_____

_____

_____

EXERCISE 7-3, Continued

C. _____

_____

_____

_____

_____

_____

_____

_____

_____

_____

_____

_____

_____

_____

_____

_____

_____

_____

_____

_____

_____

_____

_____

_____

_____

_____

_____

_____

_____

_____

_____

_____

_____

EXERCISE 7-3, Concluded

D. _____

_____

_____

_____

_____

_____

_____

_____

_____

_____

_____

_____

_____

_____

_____

_____

_____

_____

_____

_____

_____

_____

_____

_____

EXERCISE 7-4

_____

_____

_____

_____

_____

_____

_____

_____

_____

_____

_____

_____

_____

_____

_____

_____

_____

_____

_____

EXERCISE 7-5

_____

_____

_____

_____

_____

_____

_____

_____

_____

_____

_____

_____

_____

_____

_____

_____

_____

_____

_____

_____

_____

_____

_____

_____

_____

_____

_____

EXERCISE 7-6

_____

_____

_____

_____

_____

_____

_____

_____

_____

_____

_____

_____

_____

_____

_____

_____

_____

_____

_____

_____

_____

_____

_____

_____

_____

_____

_____

_____

EXERCISE 7-7

_____

_____

_____

_____

_____

_____

_____

_____

_____

_____

_____

_____

_____

_____

_____

_____

_____

_____

_____

_____

_____

_____

_____

_____

_____

_____

_____

_____

_____

_____

_____

_____

_____

_____

_____

_____

_____

EXERCISE 7-8

A. _____

_____

_____

_____

_____

_____

_____

_____

_____

_____

B. _____

_____

_____

_____

_____

_____

_____

_____

_____

_____

_____

_____

EXERCISE 7-9

A. _____

_____

B. _____

_____

_____

_____

_____

_____

EXERCISE 7-10

_____
_____
_____
_____
_____
_____
_____
_____
_____
_____
_____
_____
_____
_____
_____
_____
_____
_____
_____
_____
_____
_____
_____
_____
_____
_____
_____
_____
_____
_____
_____
_____
_____
_____
_____
_____
_____
_____
_____
_____
_____
_____
_____
_____

EXERCISE 7-11

A. _____

_____

B. _____

_____

EXERCISE 7-12

JOURNAL   PAGE

	DATE		DESCRIPTION	POST. REF.	DEBIT	CREDIT	
1							1
2							2
3							3
4							4

EXERCISE 7-13

JOURNAL   PAGE

	DATE		DESCRIPTION	POST. REF.	DEBIT	CREDIT	
1							1
2							2
3							3
4							4

EXERCISE 7-14

EXERCISE 7-14, Concluded

EXERCISE 7-15

_____

_____

_____

_____

_____

_____

_____

_____

_____

_____

_____

_____

_____

_____

_____

_____

_____

_____

_____

_____

_____

_____

_____

EXERCISE 7-16

A. Addition to the balance per bank: _____

B. Deduction from the balance per bank: _____

C. Addition to the balance per company's records: _____

D. Deduction from the balance per company's records: _____

EXERCISE 7-17

_____

_____

_____

_____

_____

EXERCISE 7-18

A.

	Bank Reconciliation			

B. _____

_____

C. _____

_____

_____

EXERCISE 7-19

JOURNAL

PAGE

	DATE		DESCRIPTION	POST. REF.	DEBIT	CREDIT	
1							1
2							2
3							3
4							4
5							5
6							6
7							7

EXERCISE 7-20

JOURNAL

PAGE

	DATE		DESCRIPTION	POST. REF.	DEBIT	CREDIT	
1							1
2							2
3							3
4							4

EXERCISE 7-21

A.

	Bank Reconciliation		

B.

EXERCISE 7-22

A. _____

_____

_____

_____

_____

_____

_____

_____

_____

_____

_____

_____

_____

_____

_____

_____

_____

_____

_____

_____

_____

_____

_____

_____

EXERCISE 7-22, Concluded

B.

Bank Reconciliation		

EXERCISE 7-23

A. _____

_____

_____

_____

_____

_____

		Bank Reconciliation		

EXERCISE 7-23, Concluded

B.

_____
_____
_____
_____
_____
_____
_____
_____
_____
_____
_____
_____
_____
_____
_____
_____
_____
_____
_____
_____
_____
_____

EXERCISE 7-24

JOURNAL   PAGE

	DATE		DESCRIPTION	POST. REF.	DEBIT	CREDIT	
1							1
2							2
3							3
4							4
5							5
6							6
7							7
8							8
9							9
10							10

PROBLEM 7-1 ___

This Page Not Used.

PROBLEM 7-2 ___

JOURNAL

PAGE

	DATE		DESCRIPTION	POST. REF.	DEBIT	CREDIT	
1							1
2							2
3							3
4							4
5							5
6							6
7							7
8							8
9							9
10							10
11							11
12							12
13							13
14							14
15							15
16							16
17							17
18							18
19							19
20							20
21							21
22							22
23							23
24							24
25							25
26							26
27							27
28							28
29							29
30							30
31							31
32							32
33							33
34							34
35							35
36							36

This Page Not Used.

PROBLEM 7-3 ___

1.

Bank Reconciliation		

PROBLEM 7-3 ___, Concluded

2.

JOURNAL   PAGE ____

	DATE		DESCRIPTION	POST. REF.	DEBIT	CREDIT	
1							1
2							2
3							3
4							4
5							5
6							6
7							7
8							8
9							9
10							10

3.

_____

_____

PROBLEM 7-4 ___

1.

	Bank Reconciliation		

PROBLEM 7-4 ___, Concluded

2.

JOURNAL

PAGE

	DATE		DESCRIPTION	POST. REF.	DEBIT	CREDIT	
1							1
2							2
3							3
4							4
5							5
6							6
7							7
8							8
9							9
10							10
11							11
12							12
13							13
14							14
15							15
16							16
17							17
18							18
19							19
20							20

3.

_____

_____

PROBLEM 7-5 ___

1.

Bank Reconciliation		

PROBLEM 7-5 ____ , Concluded

2.

JOURNAL

PAGE

	DATE		DESCRIPTION	POST. REF.	DEBIT	CREDIT	
1							1
2							2
3							3
4							4
5							5
6							6
7							7
8							8
9							9
10							10
11							11
12							12
13							13
14							14
15							15
16							16
17							17
18							18
19							19
20							20
21							21
22							22
23							23
24							24

3.

4.

_____

_____

_____

_____

_____

EXERCISE 8-1

_____
_____
_____
_____
_____
_____
_____
_____
_____
_____

EXERCISE 8-2

A. MGM Resorts International: _____

_____

B. Johnson & Johnson: _____

_____

C. _____

_____
_____
_____
_____
_____
_____
_____
_____
_____
_____

EXERCISE 8-3

JOURNAL

PAGE

	DATE		DESCRIPTION	POST. REF.	DEBIT	CREDIT	
1							1
2							2
3							3
4							4
5							5
6							6
7							7
8							8
9							9
10							10
11							11
12							12
13							13
14							14
15							15
16							16
17							17
18							18
19							19
20							20

EXERCISE 8-4

JOURNAL   PAGE

	DATE	DESCRIPTION	POST. REF.	DEBIT	CREDIT	
1						1
2						2
3						3
4						4
5						5
6						6
7						7
8						8
9						9
10						10
11						11
12						12
13						13
14						14
15						15
16						16
17						17
18						18
19						19
20						20
21						21
22						22

EXERCISE 8-5

A. and B.

JOURNAL   PAGE

	DATE	DESCRIPTION	POST. REF.	DEBIT	CREDIT	
1						1
2						2
3						3
4						4
5						5
6						6
7						7
8						8

EXERCISE 8-6

A. _____

B. _____

C. _____

D. _____

EXERCISE 8-7

Account	Due Date	Number of Days Past Due
Avalanche Auto	August 8	_____
Bales Auto	October 11	_____
Derby Auto Repair	June 23	_____
Lucky's Auto Repair	September 2	_____
Pit Stop Auto	September 19	_____
Reliable Auto Repair	July 15	_____
Trident Auto	August 24	_____
Valley Repair & Tow	May 17	_____

EXERCISE 8-8

A.

Customer	Due Date	Number of Days Past Due
Boyd Industries	April 7	_____
Hodges Company	May 29	_____
Kent Creek Inc.	June 8	_____
Lockwood Company	August 10	_____
Van Epps Company	July 2	_____

EXERCISE 8-8, Concluded

B.

	A	B	C	D	E	F	G
			Aging of Receivables Schedule				
			July 31				
1							
2						**Days Past Due**	
3	Customer	Balance	Not Past Due	1–30	31–60	61–90	Over 90
4	Acme Industries Inc.	3,000	3,000				
5							
6	Alliance Company	4,500		4,500			
21	Zollinger Company	5,000			5,000		
22	Subtotals	1,050,000	600,000	220,000	115,000	85,000	30,000
23							
24							
25							
26							
27							
28							
29							
30							

EXERCISE 8-9

			DAYS PAST DUE		
	BALANCE	NOT PAST DUE	1–30	31–60	61–90	OVER 90

EXERCISE 8-10

JOURNAL

PAGE

	DATE		DESCRIPTION	POST. REF.	DEBIT	CREDIT	
1							1
2							2
3							3
4							4
5							5
6							6
7							7

EXERCISE 8-11

Age Interval	Balance	Estimated Uncollectible Accounts	
		Percent	Amount
Not past due..................................	$892,000	0.75%	$ _____
1–30 days past due...........................	285,000	1.00	_____
31–60 days past due	101,000	8.00	_____
61–90 days past due........................	63,000	16.00	_____
91–180 days past due.......................	43,100	50.00	_____
Over 180 days past due.....................	17,700	80.00	_____
Total...	$1,401,800		$ _____

EXERCISE 8-12

JOURNAL

PAGE

	DATE		DESCRIPTION	POST. REF.	DEBIT	CREDIT	
1							1
2							2
3							3
4							4
5							5
6							6
7							7

EXERCISE 8-13

A.

JOURNAL

PAGE

	DATE		DESCRIPTION	POST. REF.	DEBIT	CREDIT	
1							1
2							2
3							3
4							4
5							5
6							6
7							7
8							8
9							9
10							10
11							11
12							12
13							13
14							14
15							15
16							16
17							17
18							18
19							19
20							20
21							21
22							22
23							23
24							24
25							25
26							26
27							27
28							28
29							29
30							30
31							31
32							32
33							33
34							34
35							35

EXERCISE 8-13, Continued

B.

JOURNAL   PAGE

	DATE		DESCRIPTION	POST. REF.	DEBIT	CREDIT	
1							1
2							2
3							3
4							4
5							5
6							6
7							7
8							8
9							9
10							10
11							11
12							12
13							13
14							14
15							15
16							16
17							17
18							18
19							19
20							20
21							21
22							22
23							23
24							24
25							25
26							26
27							27
28							28
29							29
30							30
31							31
32							32
33							33
34							34
35							35

EXERCISE 8-13, Concluded

C.

EXERCISE 8-14

A.

JOURNAL

PAGE

	DATE	DESCRIPTION	POST. REF.	DEBIT	CREDIT	
1						1
2						2
3						3
4						4
5						5
6						6
7						7
8						8
9						9
10						10
11						11
12						12
13						13
14						14
15						15
16						16
17						17
18						18
19						19
20						20
21						21
22						22
23						23
24						24
25						25
26						26
27						27
28						28
29						29
30						30
31						31
32						32
33						33
34						34
35						35

EXERCISE 8-14, Continued

B.

JOURNAL   PAGE _____

	DATE		DESCRIPTION	POST. REF.	DEBIT	CREDIT	
1							1
2							2
3							3
4							4
5							5
6							6
7							7
8							8
9							9
10							10
11							11
12							12
13							13
14							14
15							15
16							16
17							17
18							18
19							19
20							20
21							21
22							22
23							23
24							24
25							25
26							26
27							27
28							28
29							29
30							30
31							31
32							32
33							33
34							34
35							35

EXERCISE 8-14, Concluded

Computations:

Aging Class (Number of Days Past Due)	Receivables Balance on December 31	Estimated Doubtful Accounts	
		Percent	Amount
0–30 days..	$320,000	1%	$ _____
31–60 days	110,000	3	_____
61–90 days......................................	24,000	10	_____
91–120 days....................................	18,000	33	_____
More than 120 days	43,000	75	_____
Total receivables...........................	$515,000		
			$ _____

C.

EXERCISE 8-15

EXERCISE 8-16

A. _____

B. _____

EXERCISE 8-17

A.

JOURNAL   PAGE

	DATE	DESCRIPTION	POST. REF.	DEBIT	CREDIT	
1						1
2						2
3						3
4						4
5						5
6						6
7						7
8						8
9						9
10						10

B.

JOURNAL   PAGE

	DATE	DESCRIPTION	POST. REF.	DEBIT	CREDIT	
1						1
2						2
3						3
4						4
5						5
6						6
7						7
8						8
9						9
10						10
11						11
12						12
13						13
14						14
15						15
16						16

EXERCISE 8-17, Concluded

C. _____

_____

_____

_____

_____

_____

EXERCISE 8-18

A.

JOURNAL   PAGE

	DATE		DESCRIPTION	POST. REF.	DEBIT	CREDIT	
1							1
2							2
3							3
4							4
5							5
6							6
7							7
8							8
9							9
10							10

EXERCISE 8-18, Concluded

B.

	DATE		DESCRIPTION	POST. REF.	DEBIT	CREDIT	
1							1
2							2
3							3
4							4
5							5
6							6
7							7
8							8
9							9
10							10
11							11
12							12
13							13
14							14
15							15
16							16

JOURNAL   PAGE

Computations:

Aging Class (Number of Days Past Due)	Receivables Balance on December 31	Estimated Doubtful Accounts	
		Percent	Amount
0–30 days	$ 715,000	1%	$
31–60 days	310,000	2	
61–90 days	102,000	15	
91–120 days	76,000	30	
More than 120 days	97,000	60	
Total receivables	$1,300,000		
			$

EXERCISE 8-18, Concluded

C. _____

_____

_____

_____

_____

_____

_____

EXERCISE 8-19

	Date of Note	Face Amount	Interest Rate	Term of Note	Due Date	Interest Due
A.	January 3	$80,000	6%	120 days	_____	$ _____
B.	February 20	27,000	4	30 days	_____	_____
C.	May 24	62,500	8	45 days	_____	_____
D.	August 30	30,000	5	90 days	_____	_____
E.	October 4	40,000	7	90 days	_____	_____

EXERCISE 8-20

A. _____

B. _____

C. (1) and (2)

JOURNAL   PAGE _____

	DATE		DESCRIPTION	POST. REF.	DEBIT	CREDIT	
1							1
2							2
3							3
4							4
5							5
6							6
7							7

EXERCISE 8-21

A. _____

B. _____

C. _____

D. _____

_____

E. _____

_____

EXERCISE 8-22

JOURNAL   PAGE

	DATE		DESCRIPTION	POST. REF.	DEBIT	CREDIT	
1							1
2							2
3							3
4							4
5							5
6							6
7							7
8							8
9							9
10							10
11							11
12							12
13							13
14							14
15							15
16							16
17							17
18							18
19							19
20							20
21							21
22							22
23							23
24							24

EXERCISE 8-23

JOURNAL

PAGE

	DATE	DESCRIPTION	POST. REF.	DEBIT	CREDIT	
1						1
2						2
3						3
4						4
5						5
6						6
7						7
8						8
9						9
10						10
11						11
12						12
13						13
14						14
15						15
16						16
17						17
18						18

EXERCISE 8-24

JOURNAL

	DATE		DESCRIPTION	POST. REF.	DEBIT	CREDIT	
1							1
2							2
3							3
4							4
5							5
6							6
7							7
8							8
9							9
10							10
11							11
12							12
13							13
14							14
15							15
16							16
17							17
18							18
19							19
20							20
21							21
22							22
23							23
24							24
25							25
26							26
27							27
28							28
29							29
30							30

EXERCISE 8-25

_____

_____

_____

_____

_____

_____

(Optional)

_____

Balance Sheet		

PROBLEM 8-1 ___

1. and 2.

Allowance for Doubtful Accounts

_____ | _____
_____ | _____
_____ | _____
_____ | _____
_____ | _____
_____ | _____
_____ | _____
_____ | _____

Bad Debt Expense

_____ | _____
_____ | _____
_____ | _____
_____ | _____
_____ | _____

3. _____

4. A. _____

   B. _____

   C. _____

PROBLEM 8-1 ___, Continued

2.

JOURNAL   PAGE

	DATE		DESCRIPTION	POST. REF.	DEBIT	CREDIT	
1							1
2							2
3							3
4							4
5							5
6							6
7							7
8							8
9							9
10							10
11							11
12							12
13							13
14							14
15							15
16							16
17							17
18							18
19							19
20							20
21							21
22							22
23							23
24							24
25							25
26							26
27							27
28							28
29							29
30							30
31							31
32							32
33							33
34							34
35							35

PROBLEM 8-1 ___ , Concluded

JOURNAL

	DATE		DESCRIPTION	POST. REF.	DEBIT	CREDIT	
1							1
2							2
3							3
4							4
5							5
6							6
7							7
8							8
9							9
10							10
11							11
12							12
13							13
14							14
15							15
16							16
17							17
18							18
19							19
20							20
21							21
22							22
23							23
24							24
25							25
26							26
27							27
28							28
29							29
30							30
31							31
32							32
33							33
34							34
35							35
36							36

This Page Not Used.

PROBLEM 8-2 ___

1.

Customer	Due Date	Number of Days Past Due

4.

JOURNAL   PAGE

	DATE		DESCRIPTION	POST. REF.	DEBIT	CREDIT	
1							1
2							2
3							3
4							4
5							5
6							6
7							7
8							8

5. _____

_____

_____

_____

_____

_____

_____

_____

PROBLEM 8-2 ____, Concluded

2. and 3.

	A	B	C	D	E	F	G	H
1	Aging of Receivables Schedule							
2	December 31, 20Y__							
3			Not Past Due	Days Past Due				
4	Customer	Balance		1–30	31–60	61–90	91–120	Over 120
5								
6								
30								
31	Subtotals							
32								
33								
34								
35								
36								
37								
38								
39								
40								
41								
42								
43								
44								
45								
46								

PROBLEM 8-3 ___

1.

Year	Bad Debt Expense			Balance of Allowance Account, End of Year
	Expense Actually Reported	Expense Based on Estimate	Increase (Decrease) in Amount of Expense	

2. _____

_____

_____

_____

_____

_____

_____

_____

_____

_____

_____

_____

_____

_____

_____

This Page Not Used.

PROBLEM 8-4 ___

1.

Note	(A) Due Date	(B) Interest Due at Maturity
1.		
2.		
3.		
4.		
5.		
6.		

2., 3., and 4.

JOURNAL   PAGE

	DATE		DESCRIPTION	POST. REF.	DEBIT	CREDIT	
1							1
2							2
3							3
4							4
5							5
6							6
7							7
8							8
9							9
10							10
11							11
12							12
13							13
14							14
15							15
16							16
17							17
18							18
19							19
20							20
21							21
22							22
23							23
24							24

This Page Not Used.

PROBLEM 8-5 ___

		JOURNAL			PAGE

	DATE	DESCRIPTION	POST. REF.	DEBIT	CREDIT	
1						1
2						2
3						3
4						4
5						5
6						6
7						7
8						8
9						9
10						10
11						11
12						12
13						13
14						14
15						15
16						16
17						17
18						18
19						19
20						20
21						21
22						22
23						23
24						24
25						25
26						26
27						27
28						28
29						29
30						30
31						31
32						32
33						33
34						34
35						35
36						36

This Page Not Used.

PROBLEM 8-6 ___

JOURNAL

PAGE

	DATE		DESCRIPTION	POST. REF.	DEBIT	CREDIT	
1							1
2							2
3							3
4							4
5							5
6							6
7							7
8							8
9							9
10							10
11							11
12							12
13							13
14							14
15							15
16							16
17							17
18							18
19							19
20							20
21							21
22							22
23							23
24							24
25							25
26							26
27							27
28							28
29							29
30							30
31							31
32							32
33							33
34							34
35							35
36							36

PROBLEM 8-6 ___, Concluded

JOURNAL

	DATE		DESCRIPTION	POST. REF.	DEBIT	CREDIT	
1							1
2							2
3							3
4							4
5							5
6							6
7							7
8							8
9							9
10							10
11							11
12							12
13							13
14							14
15							15
16							16
17							17
18							18
19							19
20							20
21							21
22							22
23							23
24							24
25							25
26							26
27							27
28							28
29							29
30							30
31							31
32							32
33							33
34							34
35							35
36							36

EXERCISE 9-1

A. New printing press costs debited to the asset account: _____

_____

_____

_____

_____

B. Used printing press costs debited to the asset account: _____

_____

_____

_____

_____

EXERCISE 9-2

A. _____

_____

_____

B. _____

_____

EXERCISE 9-3

EXERCISE 9-4

A. _____

_____

_____

_____

_____

B. _____

_____

_____

_____

_____

EXERCISE 9-5

A. 4 years: _____

B. 8 years: _____

C. 10 years: _____

D. 16 years: _____

E. 25 years: _____

F. 40 years: _____

G. 50 years: _____

EXERCISE 9-6

_____

_____

EXERCISE 9-7

_____

_____

_____

_____

EXERCISE 9-8

A.

Truck No.	Rate per Mile	Miles Operated	Credit to Accumulated Depreciation
1	_____	_____	$_____
2	_____	_____	$_____
3	_____	_____	$_____
4	_____	_____	$_____
Total			$_____

B.

JOURNAL   PAGE

	DATE		DESCRIPTION	POST. REF.	DEBIT	CREDIT	
1							1
2							2
3							3
4							4
5							5

EXERCISE 9-9

A. Straight-line method:

First year: _____

Second year: _____

B. Double-declining-balance method:

First year: _____

Second year: _____

EXERCISE 9-10

A. Straight-line method:

_____

B. Double-declining-balance method:

Year 1: _____

Year 2: _____

EXERCISE 9-11

A. Straight-line method:

Year 1: _____

Year 2: _____

B. Double-declining-balance method:

Year 1: _____

Year 2: _____

EXERCISE 9-12

A. _____

B. _____

C. _____

EXERCISE 9-13

1. _____

2. _____

3. _____

4. _____

5. _____

6. _____

7. _____

8. _____

9. _____

10. _____

EXERCISE 9-14

1. _____

2. _____

3. _____

4. _____

5. _____

6. _____

7. _____

8. _____

9. _____

10. _____

EXERCISE 9-15

JOURNAL PAGE

	DATE	DESCRIPTION	POST. REF.	DEBIT	CREDIT	
1						1
2						2
3						3
4						4
5						5
6						6
7						7
8						8
9						9
10						10
11						11
12						12

EXERCISE 9-16

A. and B.

JOURNAL PAGE

	DATE	DESCRIPTION	POST. REF.	DEBIT	CREDIT	
1						1
2						2
3						3
4						4
5						5
6						6
7						7
8						8
9						9
10						10

EXERCISE 9-17

A.

B. (1) and (2)

JOURNAL

PAGE

	DATE		DESCRIPTION	POST. REF.	DEBIT	CREDIT	
1							1
2							2
3							3
4							4
5							5
6							6
7							7
8							8
9							9
10							10
11							11
12							12
13							13
14							14

EXERCISE 9-18

A. Year 1: _____

Year 2: _____

Year 3: _____

B. _____

EXERCISE 9-18, Concluded

C. and D.

JOURNAL   PAGE _____

	DATE		DESCRIPTION	POST. REF.	DEBIT	CREDIT	
1							1
2							2
3							3
4							4
5							5
6							6
7							7
8							8
9							9
10							10
11							11
12							12
13							13
14							14

EXERCISE 9-19

A. _____

_____

B.

JOURNAL   PAGE _____

	DATE		DESCRIPTION	POST. REF.	DEBIT	CREDIT	
1							1
2							2
3							3
4							4
5							5

EXERCISE 9-20

A. _____

_____

B.

JOURNAL   PAGE

	DATE		DESCRIPTION	POST. REF.	DEBIT	CREDIT	
1							1
2							2
3							3
4							4
5							5

EXERCISE 9-21

A.

	CURRENT YEAR	PRECEDING YEAR	

_____

_____

_____

_____

_____

_____

_____

_____

_____

_____

_____

EXERCISE 9-21, Concluded

B. _____

_____

_____

_____

_____

_____

_____

_____

_____

_____

EXERCISE 9-22

_____

_____

_____

_____

_____

_____

_____

_____

_____

_____

_____

APPENDIX EXERCISE 9-23

A.

B.

APPENDIX EXERCISE 9-24

A.

B.

APPENDIX EXERCISE 9-25

A. and B.

JOURNAL   PAGE _____

	DATE		DESCRIPTION	POST. REF.	DEBIT	CREDIT	
1							1
2							2
3							3
4							4
5							5
6							6
7							7
8							8
9							9
10							10
11							11
12							12
13							13
14							14

APPENDIX EXERCISE 9-26

A. and B.

JOURNAL   PAGE _____

	DATE		DESCRIPTION	POST. REF.	DEBIT	CREDIT	
1							1
2							2
3							3
4							4
5							5
6							6
7							7
8							8
9							9
10							10
11							11
12							12
13							13
14							14

This Page Not Used.

PROBLEM 9-1 ___

1. and 2.

Item	Land	Land Improvements	Building	Other Accounts
A.				
B.				
C.				
D.				
E.				
F.				
G.				
H.				
I.				
J.				
K.				
L.				
M.				
N.				
O.				
P.				
Q.				
R.				
S.				
Total				

PROBLEM 9-1 ___ , Concluded

3. _____

_____

_____

_____

_____

_____

4. _____

_____

_____

_____

_____

_____

_____

_____

_____

_____

_____

PROBLEM 9-2 ___

1.

Depreciation Expense

Year	A. Straight-Line Method	B. Units-of-Activity Method	C. Double-Declining-Balance Method
Total			

Supporting Calculations:

_____

_____

_____

_____

_____

_____

_____

_____

_____

_____

_____

_____

_____

_____

_____

_____

2. _____

_____

3. _____

_____

_____

_____

This Page Not Used.

PROBLEM 9-3 ___

A.

Straight-Line Method

Year	Calculations	Depreciation Expense
1		
2		
3		
4		

B.

Units-of-Activity Method

Year	Calculations	Depreciation Expense
1		
2		
3		
4		

C.

Double-Declining-Balance Method

Year	Calculations	Depreciation Expense
1		
2		
3		
4		

This Page Not Used.

PROBLEM 9-4 ___

1. A.

Straight-Line Method

Year	Depreciation Expense	Accumulated Depreciation, End of Year	Book Value, End of Year
1			
2			
3			
4			
5			

B.

Double-Declining-Balance Method

Year	Depreciation Expense	Accumulated Depreciation, End of Year	Book Value, End of Year
1			
2			
3			
4			
5			

PROBLEM 9-4 ___ , Concluded

2.

JOURNAL   PAGE

	DATE		DESCRIPTION	POST. REF.	DEBIT	CREDIT	
1							1
2							2
3							3
4							4
5							5
6							6
7							7

3.

JOURNAL   PAGE

	DATE		DESCRIPTION	POST. REF.	DEBIT	CREDIT	
1							1
2							2
3							3
4							4
5							5
6							6
7							7

PROBLEM 9-5 ___

JOURNAL   PAGE

	DATE		DESCRIPTION	POST. REF.	DEBIT	CREDIT	
1							1
2							2
3							3
4							4
5							5
6							6
7							7
8							8
9							9
10							10
11							11
12							12
13							13
14							14
15							15
16							16
17							17
18							18
19							19
20							20
21							21
22							22
23							23
24							24
25							25
26							26
27							27
28							28
29							29
30							30
31							31
32							32
33							33
34							34
35							35
36							36

PROBLEM 9-5 ___ , Concluded

JOURNAL

	DATE		DESCRIPTION	POST. REF.	DEBIT	CREDIT	
1							1
2							2
3							3
4							4
5							5
6							6
7							7
8							8
9							9
10							10
11							11
12							12
13							13
14							14
15							15
16							16
17							17
18							18
19							19
20							20
21							21
22							22
23							23
24							24
25							25
26							26
27							27
28							28
29							29
30							30
31							31
32							32
33							33
34							34
35							35
36							36

PROBLEM 9-6 ___

1. A. _____

_____

_____

B. _____

_____

_____

C. _____

_____

_____

2.

JOURNAL

PAGE

	DATE		DESCRIPTION	POST. REF.	DEBIT	CREDIT	
1							1
2							2
3							3
4							4
5							5
6							6
7							7
8							8
9							9
10							10
11							11
12							12
13							13
14							14
15							15

This Page Not Used.

EXERCISE 10-1

EXERCISE 10-2

A. and B.

JOURNAL   PAGE

	DATE	DESCRIPTION	POST. REF.	DEBIT	CREDIT	
1						1
2						2
3						3
4						4
5						5
6						6
7						7
8						8
9						9
10						10
11						11
12						12
13						13
14						14
15						15

EXERCISE 10-3

A. _____

_____

B. (1) _____

_____

(2) _____

_____

C. _____

_____

_____

_____

_____

_____

_____

_____

_____

_____

_____

_____

_____

_____

_____

_____

_____

_____

_____

_____

EXERCISE 10-4

A. and B.

JOURNAL   PAGE

	DATE		DESCRIPTION	POST. REF.	DEBIT	CREDIT	
1							1
2							2
3							3
4							4
5							5
6							6
7							7

EXERCISE 10-5

A. and B.

	DATE		DESCRIPTION	POST. REF.	DEBIT	CREDIT	
1							1
2							2
3							3
4							4
5							5
6							6
7							7

JOURNAL   PAGE

EXERCISE 10-6

A., B., and C.

JOURNAL   PAGE

	DATE		DESCRIPTION	POST. REF.	DEBIT	CREDIT	
1							1
2							2
3							3
4							4
5							5
6							6
7							7
8							8
9							9
10							10
11							11
12							12
13							13
14							14
15							15
16							16
17							17
18							18

EXERCISE 10-7

A. _____

_____

B. _____

_____

C. _____

_____

EXERCISE 10-8

A.

B.

EXERCISE 10-9

	Consultant	Computer Programmer	Administrator
Regular earnings.....................................	$	$	$
Overtime earnings....................................			
Gross pay..	$	$	$
Deductions:			
Social security tax............................	$	$	$
Medicare tax			
Federal income tax withheld................			
Total deductions	$	$	$
Net pay...	$	$	$

EXERCISE 10-10

A.

EXERCISE 10-10, Concluded

B. and C.

JOURNAL   PAGE

	DATE		DESCRIPTION	POST. REF.	DEBIT	CREDIT	
1							1
2							2
3							3
4							4
5							5
6							6
7							7
8							8
9							9
10							10
11							11
12							12
13							13
14							14
15							15
16							16

EXERCISE 10-11

A.

EXERCISE 10-11, Concluded

B.

JOURNAL

PAGE

	DATE		DESCRIPTION	POST. REF.	DEBIT	CREDIT	
1							1
2							2
3							3
4							4
5							5
6							6
7							7
8							8
9							9

EXERCISE 10-12

A. and B.

JOURNAL

PAGE

	DATE		DESCRIPTION	POST. REF.	DEBIT	CREDIT	
1							1
2							2
3							3
4							4
5							5
6							6
7							7
8							8
9							9
10							10
11							11
12							12
13							13
14							14
15							15
16							16
17							17
18							18
19							19
20							20

EXERCISE 10-13

A. and B.

JOURNAL   PAGE

	DATE		DESCRIPTION	POST. REF.	DEBIT	CREDIT	
1							1
2							2
3							3
4							4
5							5
6							6
7							7
8							8
9							9
10							10
11							11
12							12
13							13
14							14
15							15
16							16
17							17
18							18
19							19
20							20
21							21
22							22

EXERCISE 10-14

_____

_____

_____

_____

_____

_____

_____

_____

_____

_____

EXERCISE 10-15

A. _____
_____
_____
_____
_____
_____

B. _____
_____
_____
_____
_____
_____

C. _____
_____
_____
_____
_____
_____

D. _____
_____
_____
_____
_____
_____

E. _____
_____
_____
_____
_____
_____

EXERCISE 10-16

A.

		JOURNAL				PAGE

	DATE		DESCRIPTION	POST. REF.	DEBIT	CREDIT	
1							1
2							2
3							3
4							4
5							5

B. _____

_____

_____

_____

_____

_____

_____

EXERCISE 10-17

A.

		JOURNAL				PAGE

	DATE		DESCRIPTION	POST. REF.	DEBIT	CREDIT	
1							1
2							2
3							3
4							4
5							5
6							6
7							7
8							8

EXERCISE 10-17, Concluded

B. _____

_____

_____

_____

_____

_____

_____

_____

_____

_____

_____

_____

EXERCISE 10-18

_____

_____

_____

_____

_____

_____

_____

_____

_____

_____

_____

_____

_____

_____

_____

_____

_____

_____

EXERCISE 10-19

A. (1) and (2)

JOURNAL

PAGE

	DATE		DESCRIPTION	POST. REF.	DEBIT	CREDIT	
1							1
2							2
3							3
4							4
5							5
6							6
7							7

B. _____

_____

_____

_____

_____

_____

_____

_____

_____

_____

_____

_____

Supporting Calculations:

EXERCISE 10-20

JOURNAL   PAGE

	DATE		DESCRIPTION	POST. REF.	DEBIT	CREDIT	
1							1
2							2
3							3
4							4
5							5
6							6
7							7
8							8
9							9
10							10
11							11
12							12
13							13
14							14
15							15

EXERCISE 10-21

A.

For the Year Ending December 31	A January 1 Carrying Amount	B Note Payment (Cash Paid)	C Interest Expense (7% of January 1 Note Carrying Amount)	D Decrease in Notes Payable (B – C)	E December 31 Carrying Amount (A – D)

EXERCISE 10-21, Concluded

B.

JOURNAL PAGE

	DATE		DESCRIPTION	POST. REF.	DEBIT	CREDIT	
1							1
2							2
3							3
4							4
5							5
6							6
7							7
8							8
9							9
10							10
11							11
12							12
13							13
14							14
15							15
16							16
17							17
18							18
19							19
20							20
21							21
22							22
23							23
24							24
25							25

C. _____

_____

EXERCISE 10-22

A. and B.

JOURNAL PAGE

	DATE		DESCRIPTION	POST. REF.	DEBIT	CREDIT	
1							1
2							2
3							3
4							4
5							5
6							6
7							7
8							8
9							9
10							10
11							11
12							12

EXERCISE 10-23

A. _____

_____

_____

_____

_____

_____

_____

_____

_____

_____

_____

B.

JOURNAL PAGE

	DATE		DESCRIPTION	POST. REF.	DEBIT	CREDIT	
1							1
2							2
3							3
4							4

EXERCISE 10-23, Concluded

C. _____

_____

_____

_____

_____

_____

EXERCISE 10-24

A.

JOURNAL   PAGE

	DATE		DESCRIPTION	POST. REF.	DEBIT	CREDIT	
1							1
2							2
3							3
4							4
5							5

B. _____

_____

_____

_____

_____

_____

_____

_____

_____

_____

_____

_____

_____

_____

_____

_____

_____

_____

_____

_____

PROBLEM 10-1 ___

1.

JOURNAL   PAGE

	DATE	DESCRIPTION	POST. REF.	DEBIT	CREDIT	
1						1
2						2
3						3
4						4
5						5
6						6
7						7
8						8
9						9
10						10
11						11
12						12
13						13
14						14
15						15
16						16
17						17
18						18
19						19
20						20
21						21
22						22
23						23
24						24
25						25
26						26
27						27
28						28
29						29
30						30
31						31
32						32
33						33
34						34
35						35

PROBLEM 10-1 ___ , Continued

JOURNAL   PAGE

	DATE	DESCRIPTION	POST. REF.	DEBIT	CREDIT	
1						1
2						2
3						3
4						4
5						5
6						6
7						7
8						8
9						9
10						10
11						11
12						12
13						13
14						14
15						15
16						16
17						17
18						18
19						19
20						20
21						21
22						22
23						23
24						24
25						25
26						26
27						27
28						28
29						29
30						30
31						31
32						32
33						33
34						34
35						35
36						36

PROBLEM 10-1 ___ , Concluded

2. A. and B.

JOURNAL   PAGE

	DATE		DESCRIPTION	POST. REF.	DEBIT	CREDIT	
1							1
2							2
3							3
4							4
5							5
6							6
7							7
8							8
9							9
10							10
11							11
12							12
13							13
14							14
15							15
16							16
17							17
18							18
19							19
20							20
21							21
22							22
23							23
24							24
25							25
26							26
27							27
28							28
29							29
30							30
31							31
32							32
33							33
34							34
35							35

This Page Not Used.

PROBLEM 10-2 ___

1. A. and B.

JOURNAL   PAGE

	DATE		DESCRIPTION	POST. REF.	DEBIT	CREDIT	
1							1
2							2
3							3
4							4
5							5
6							6
7							7
8							8
9							9
10							10
11							11
12							12
13							13
14							14
15							15
16							16
17							17
18							18
19							19
20							20
21							21
22							22
23							23
24							24
25							25
26							26
27							27
28							28
29							29
30							30
31							31
32							32
33							33
34							34
35							35

PROBLEM 10-2 ___, Concluded

2. A. and B.

JOURNAL

PAGE

	DATE		DESCRIPTION	POST. REF.	DEBIT	CREDIT	
1							1
2							2
3							3
4							4
5							5
6							6
7							7
8							8
9							9
10							10
11							11
12							12
13							13
14							14
15							15
16							16
17							17
18							18
19							19
20							20
21							21
22							22
23							23
24							24
25							25
26							26
27							27
28							28
29							29
30							30
31							31
32							32
33							33
34							34
35							35

PROBLEM 10-3 ___

1.

Employee	Gross Earnings	Federal Income Tax Withheld	Social Security Tax Withheld	Medicare Tax Withheld

PROBLEM 10-3 ___ , Concluded

2. Payroll taxes incurred and paid by employer:

   A. Social security tax paid by employer............................ $ _____

   B. Medicare tax paid by employer ....   _____

   C. State unemployment compensation tax ....   _____

   Calculations and comments:

   _____

   _____

   _____

   _____

   _____

   _____

   _____

   _____

   D. Federal unemployment compensation tax ....   _____

   E. Total payroll tax expense .... $ _____

PROBLEM 10-4 ___

1.

PAYROLL FOR WEEK ENDING *December 9*

EMPLOYEE	TOTAL HOURS	EARNINGS			DEDUCTIONS					PAID		ACCOUNTS DEBITED	
		REGULAR	OVERTIME	TOTAL	SOCIAL SECURITY TAX	MEDICARE TAX	FEDERAL INCOME TAX	U.S. SAVINGS BONDS	TOTAL	NET PAY	CK. NO.	SALES SALARIES EXPENSE	OFFICE SALARIES EXPENSE
1													
2													
3													
4													
5													
6													
7													
8													
9													
10													
11													
12													

PROBLEM 10-4 ___ , Concluded

2.

JOURNAL

	DATE		DESCRIPTION	POST. REF.	DEBIT	CREDIT	
1							1
2							2
3							3
4							4
5							5
6							6
7							7
8							8
9							9
10							10
11							11
12							12

PROBLEM 10-5 ___

1.

JOURNAL					PAGE

	DATE	DESCRIPTION	POST. REF.	DEBIT	CREDIT	
1						1
2						2
3						3
4						4
5						5
6						6
7						7
8						8
9						9
10						10
11						11
12						12
13						13
14						14
15						15
16						16
17						17
18						18
19						19
20						20
21						21
22						22
23						23
24						24
25						25
26						26
27						27
28						28
29						29
30						30
31						31
32						32
33						33
34						34
35						35

PROBLEM 10-5 ___, Continued

JOURNAL

PAGE

	DATE		DESCRIPTION	POST. REF.	DEBIT	CREDIT	
1							1
2							2
3							3
4							4
5							5
6							6
7							7
8							8
9							9
10							10
11							11
12							12
13							13
14							14
15							15
16							16
17							17
18							18
19							19
20							20
21							21
22							22
23							23
24							24
25							25
26							26
27							27
28							28
29							29
30							30
31							31
32							32
33							33
34							34
35							35
36							36

PROBLEM 10-5 ___ , Continued

JOURNAL   PAGE

	DATE	DESCRIPTION	POST. REF.	DEBIT	CREDIT	
1						1
2						2
3						3
4						4
5						5
6						6
7						7
8						8
9						9
10						10
11						11
12						12
13						13
14						14
15						15
16						16
17						17
18						18
19						19
20						20
21						21
22						22
23						23
24						24
25						25
26						26
27						27
28						28
29						29
30						30
31						31
32						32
33						33
34						34
35						35
36						36

PROBLEM 10-5 ___ , Concluded

2. A. and B.

JOURNAL

	DATE		DESCRIPTION	POST. REF.	DEBIT	CREDIT	
1							1
2							2
3							3
4							4
5							5
6							6
7							7
8							8
9							9
10							10
11							11
12							12
13							13
14							14
15							15
16							16
17							17
18							18
19							19
20							20
21							21
22							22
23							23
24							24
25							25
26							26
27							27
28							28
29							29
30							30
31							31
32							32
33							33
34							34
35							35

COMPREHENSIVE PROBLEM 3

1.

JOURNAL

PAGE

	DATE	DESCRIPTION	POST. REF.	DEBIT	CREDIT	
1						1
2						2
3						3
4						4
5						5
6						6
7						7
8						8
9						9
10						10
11						11
12						12
13						13
14						14
15						15
16						16
17						17
18						18
19						19
20						20
21						21
22						22
23						23
24						24
25						25
26						26
27						27
28						28
29						29
30						30
31						31
32						32
33						33
34						34
35						35

COMPREHENSIVE PROBLEM 3, Continued

JOURNAL

	DATE		DESCRIPTION	POST. REF.	DEBIT	CREDIT	
1							1
2							2
3							3
4							4
5							5
6							6
7							7
8							8
9							9
10							10
11							11
12							12
13							13
14							14
15							15
16							16
17							17
18							18
19							19
20							20
21							21
22							22
23							23
24							24
25							25
26							26
27							27
28							28
29							29
30							30
31							31
32							32
33							33
34							34
35							35
36							36

COMPREHENSIVE PROBLEM 3, Continued

	DATE	DESCRIPTION	POST. REF.	DEBIT	CREDIT	
1						1
2						2
3						3
4						4
5						5
6						6
7						7
8						8
9						9
10						10
11						11
12						12
13						13
14						14
15						15
16						16
17						17
18						18
19						19
20						20
21						21
22						22
23						23
24						24
25						25
26						26
27						27
28						28
29						29
30						30
31						31
32						32
33						33
34						34
35						35
36						36

COMPREHENSIVE PROBLEM 3, Continued

2.

Bank Reconciliation

3.

JOURNAL

	DATE	DESCRIPTION	POST. REF.	DEBIT	CREDIT	
1						1
2						2
3						3
4						4
5						5

COMPREHENSIVE PROBLEM 3, Continued

4. A. through J.

JOURNAL   PAGE

	DATE	DESCRIPTION	POST. REF.	DEBIT	CREDIT	
1						1
2						2
3						3
4						4
5						5
6						6
7						7
8						8
9						9
10						10
11						11
12						12
13						13
14						14
15						15
16						16
17						17
18						18
19						19
20						20
21						21
22						22
23						23
24						24
25						25
26						26
27						27
28						28
29						29
30						30
31						31
32						32
33						33
34						34
35						35

COMPREHENSIVE PROBLEM 3, Continued

JOURNAL

	DATE		DESCRIPTION	POST. REF.	DEBIT	CREDIT	
1							1
2							2
3							3
4							4
5							5
6							6
7							7
8							8
9							9
10							10
11							11
12							12
13							13
14							14
15							15
16							16
17							17
18							18
19							19
20							20
21							21
22							22
23							23
24							24
25							25
26							26
27							27
28							28
29							29
30							30
31							31
32							32
33							33
34							34
35							35
36							36

COMPREHENSIVE PROBLEM 3, Continued

5.

Balance Sheet			

COMPREHENSIVE PROBLEM 3, Continued

Balance Sheet (continued)

COMPREHENSIVE PROBLEM 3, Concluded

Balance Sheet (continued)

This Page Not Used.

EXERCISE 11-1

_____

_____

_____

_____

_____

_____

_____

_____

EXERCISE 11-2

JOURNAL PAGE _____

	DATE		DESCRIPTION	POST. REF.	DEBIT	CREDIT	
1							1
2							2
3							3
4							4
5							5
6							6
7							7
8							8
9							9

EXERCISE 11-3

A. 1., 2., and 3.

JOURNAL   PAGE

	DATE		DESCRIPTION	POST. REF.	DEBIT	CREDIT	
1							1
2							2
3							3
4							4
5							5
6							6
7							7
8							8
9							9
10							10
11							11
12							12
13							13
14							14
15							15

B.

C.

EXERCISE 11-4

A. and B.

JOURNAL   PAGE

	DATE		DESCRIPTION	POST. REF.	DEBIT	CREDIT	
1							1
2							2
3							3
4							4
5							5
6							6
7							7
8							8
9							9
10							10
11							11
12							12

C. _____

_____

_____

_____

_____

_____

_____

_____

EXERCISE 11-5

JOURNAL   PAGE

	DATE		DESCRIPTION	POST. REF.	DEBIT	CREDIT	
1							1
2							2
3							3
4							4
5							5
6							6
7							7
8							8
9							9
10							10
11							11
12							12
13							13

EXERCISE 11-6

JOURNAL   PAGE

	DATE		DESCRIPTION	POST. REF.	DEBIT	CREDIT	
1							1
2							2
3							3
4							4
5							5
6							6
7							7
8							8
9							9
10							10
11							11
12							12
13							13

EXERCISE 11-7

_____
_____
_____
_____
_____
_____
_____
_____
_____

APPENDIX 1 EXERCISE 11-8

A. _____
_____

B. _____
_____
_____

APPENDIX 1 EXERCISE 11-9

A.

B. _____
_____

C. _____
_____
_____
_____

APPENDIX 1 EXERCISE 11-10

_____
_____

APPENDIX 1 EXERCISE 11-11

APPENDIX 1 EXERCISE 11-12

APPENDIX 1 EXERCISE 11-13

APPENDIX 2 EXERCISE 11-14

A. 1., 2., and 3.

JOURNAL

PAGE _____

	DATE		DESCRIPTION	POST. REF.	DEBIT	CREDIT	
1							1
2							2
3							3
4							4
5							5
6							6
7							7
8							8
9							9
10							10
11							11
12							12
13							13
14							14
15							15
16							16
17							17
18							18

B.

C. _____

_____

_____

_____

_____

_____

_____

APPENDIX 2 EXERCISE 11-15

A. 1., 2., and 3.

JOURNAL

	DATE		DESCRIPTION	POST. REF.	DEBIT	CREDIT	
1							1
2							2
3							3
4							4
5							5
6							6
7							7
8							8
9							9
10							10
11							11
12							12
13							13
14							14
15							15
16							16
17							17
18							18

B.

C. _____

_____

_____

_____

_____

_____

_____

APPENDIX 1 AND 2 EXERCISE 11-16

A., B., C., and D.

APPENDIX 1 AND 2 EXERCISE 11-17

A., B., C., and D.

PROBLEM 11-1 ___

1. and 2.

JOURNAL   PAGE

	DATE		DESCRIPTION	POST. REF.	DEBIT	CREDIT	
1							1
2							2
3							3
4							4
5							5
6							6
7							7
8							8
9							9
10							10
11							11
12							12
13							13
14							14
15							15
16							16
17							17
18							18
19							19
20							20
21							21
22							22
23							23
24							24

PROBLEM 11-1 ___, Concluded

3. _____

4. _____

_____

_____

_____

_____

_____

5.

PROBLEM 11-2 ___

1. and 2.

JOURNAL

	DATE		DESCRIPTION	POST. REF.	DEBIT	CREDIT	
1							1
2							2
3							3
4							4
5							5
6							6
7							7
8							8
9							9
10							10
11							11
12							12
13							13
14							14
15							15
16							16
17							17
18							18
19							19
20							20
21							21
22							22
23							23
24							24

PROBLEM 11-2 ___ , Concluded

3. _____

4. _____

_____

_____

_____

_____

_____

5.

PROBLEM 11-3 ___

1.

		JOURNAL				PAGE	

	DATE		DESCRIPTION	POST. REF.	DEBIT	CREDIT	
1							1
2							2
3							3
4							4
5							5
6							6
7							7
8							8
9							9
10							10
11							11
12							12
13							13
14							14
15							15
16							16
17							17
18							18
19							19
20							20
21							21
22							22
23							23
24							24
25							25
26							26
27							27
28							28
29							29
30							30
31							31
32							32
33							33
34							34
35							35

PROBLEM 11-3 ___, Concluded

2. **(A)** Year 1: _____

   (B) Year 2: _____

3.

APPENDIX 1 AND 2 PROBLEM 11-4 ___

1. and 2.

JOURNAL

	DATE		DESCRIPTION	POST. REF.	DEBIT	CREDIT	
1							1
2							2
3							3
4							4
5							5
6							6
7							7
8							8
9							9
10							10
11							11
12							12
13							13
14							14
15							15
16							16
17							17
18							18
19							19
20							20
21							21
22							22
23							23
24							24

3. _____

This Page Not Used.

APPENDIX 1 AND 2 PROBLEM 11-5 ___

1. and 2.

	DATE	DESCRIPTION	POST. REF.	DEBIT	CREDIT	
1						1
2						2
3						3
4						4
5						5
6						6
7						7
8						8
9						9
10						10
11						11
12						12
13						13
14						14
15						15
16						16
17						17
18						18
19						19
20						20
21						21
22						22
23						23
24						24

3. _____

This Page Not Used.

EXERCISE 12-1

Description	1st Year	2nd Year	3rd Year	4th Year
Total dividend declared				
Preferred dividend (current)				
Preferred dividend in arrears				
Total preferred dividends				
Preferred shares outstanding				
Preferred dividend per share				
Dividend for common shares				
Common shares outstanding				
Common dividend per share				

EXERCISE 12-2

Description	1st Year	2nd Year	3rd Year	4th Year
Total dividend declared				
Preferred dividend (current)				
Preferred dividend in arrears				
Total preferred dividends				
Preferred shares outstanding				
Preferred dividend per share				
Dividend for common shares				
Common shares outstanding				
Common dividend per share				

EXERCISE 12-3

A.

	DATE		DESCRIPTION	POST. REF.	DEBIT	CREDIT	
%							%
&							&
'							'
(							(
)							)
*							*
+							+
,							,
-							-
%.							%.
%%							%%
%&							%&
%'							%'
%(							%(
%)							%)
%*							%*
%+							%+
%,							%,

EXERCISE 12-4

A.

JOURNAL

PAGE

	DATE		DESCRIPTION	POST. REF.	DEBIT	CREDIT	
%							%
&							&
'							'
(							(
)							)
*							*
+							+
,							,
-							-
%.							%.
%%							%%
%&							%&
%'							%'
%(							%(
%)							%)
%*							%*
%+							%+
%,							%,

ııı

EXERCISE 12-5

JOURNAL

PAGE

	DATE		DESCRIPTION	POST. REF.	DEBIT	CREDIT	
%							%
&							&
'							'
(							(
)							)
*							*
+							+
,							,
-							-

EXERCISE 12-6

JOURNAL

	DATE		DESCRIPTION	POST. REF.	DEBIT	CREDIT	
%							%
&							&
'							'
(							(
)							)
*							*
+							+
'							'
-							-
%.							%.
%%							%%
%&							%&
%'							%'
%(							%(
%)							%)
%*							%*
%+							%+
%,							%,
%-							%-
&.							&.

EXERCISE 12-7

JOURNAL   PAGE _____

	DATE		DESCRIPTION	POST. REF.	DEBIT	CREDIT	
%							%
&							&
'							'
(							(
)							)
*							*
+							+
'							'
-							-
%.							%.
%%							%%
%&							%&
%'							%'
%(							%(
%)							%)
%*							%*
%+							%+
%,							%,
%-							%-
&.							&.

EXERCISE 12-8

JOURNAL

	DATE		DESCRIPTION	POST. REF.	DEBIT	CREDIT	
%							%
&							&
'							'
(							(
)							)
*							*
+							+
'							'
-							-
%.							%.
%%							%%
%&							%&
%'							%'
%(							%(
%)							%)
%*							%*
%+							%+
%,							%,
%-							%-
&.							&.
&%							&%
&&							&&
&'							&'
&(							&(
&)							&)
&*							&*

EXERCISE 12-9

JOURNAL   PAGE

	DATE		DESCRIPTION	POST. REF.	DEBIT	CREDIT	
%							%
&							&
'							'
(							(
)							)
*							*
+							+
'							'
-							-

EXERCISE 12-10

A. (1) and (2)

JOURNAL   PAGE

	DATE		DESCRIPTION	POST. REF.	DEBIT	CREDIT	
%							%
&							&
'							'
(							(
)							)
*							*
+							+
'							'
-							-
%.							%.
%%							%%
%&							%&
%'							%'
%(							%(

B. (1) Total paid-in capital: _____

    (2) Total retained earnings: _____

    (3) Total stockholders' equity: _____

C. (1) Total paid-in capital: _____

    (2) Total retained earnings: _____

    (3) Total stockholders' equity: _____

EXERCISE 12-11

!" _____

'" _____

EXERCISE 12-12

	Assets	Liabilities	Stockholders' Equity
!" Authorizing and issuing stock certificates in a stock split	_____	_____	_____
'" Declaring a stock dividend	_____	_____	_____
C. Issuing stock certificates for the stock dividend declared in (B)	_____	_____	_____
D. Declaring a cash dividend............................	_____	_____	_____
E. Paying the cash dividend declared in (D)........	_____	_____	_____

EXERCISE 12-13

JOURNAL

PAGE

	DATE		DESCRIPTION	POST. REF.	DEBIT	CREDIT	
%							%
&							&
'							'
(							(
)							)
*							*
+							+
'							'
-							-
%.							%.
%%							%%
%&							%&
%'							%'
%(							%(
%)							%)
%*							%*
%+							%+
%,							%,
%-							%-
&.							&.
&%							&%
&&							&&
&'							&'
&(							&(
&)							&)
&*							&*
&+							&+
&,							&,
&-							&-
'.							'.
'%							'%
'&							'&
"							"
'(							'(
')							')
'*							'*

EXERCISE 12-14

A.

	DATE		DESCRIPTION	POST. REF.	DEBIT	CREDIT	
%							%
&							&
'							'
(							(
)							)
*							*
+							+
'							'
-							-
%.							%.
%%							%%
%&							%&
%'							%'
%(							%(
%)							%)
%*							%*
%+							%+
%,							%,
%-							%-
&.							&.

JOURNAL PAGE

''' _____

C. _____

_____

_____

_____

_____

EXERCISE 12-15

A.

JOURNAL

PAGE

	DATE		DESCRIPTION	POST. REF.	DEBIT	CREDIT	
%							%
&							&
'							'
(							(
)							)
*							*
+							+
,							,
-							-
%.							%.
%%							%%
%&							%&
%'							%'
%(							%(
%)							%)
%*							%*
%+							%+
%,							%,
%-							%-
&.							&.

''' _____

C. _____

D. _____

_____

_____

EXERCISE 12-16

A.

JOURNAL PAGE

	DATE		DESCRIPTION	POST. REF.	DEBIT	CREDIT	
%							%
&							&
'							'
(							(
)							)
*							*
+							+
,							,
-							-
%.							%.
%%							%%
%&							%&
%'							%'
%(							%(
%)							%)
%*							%*
%+							%+
%,							%,
%-							%-
&.							&.

B. _____

C. _____

D. _____

_____

_____

_____

_____

EXERCISE 12-17

EXERCISE 12-18

EXERCISE 12-19

EXERCISE 12-20

Retained Earnings Statement

EXERCISE 12-21

EXERCISE 12-21, Concluded

EXERCISE 12-22

Statement of Stockholders' Equity

PROBLEM 12-1 ___

1.

Year	Total Dividends	Preferred Dividends		Common Dividends	
		Total	Per Share	Total	Per Share
Year 1					
Year 2					
Year 3					
Year 4					
Year 5					
Year 6					

2. Average annual dividend for preferred: _____

  Average annual dividend for common: _____

3. A. _____

  B. _____

This Page Not Used.

PROBLEM 12-2 ___

JOURNAL

	DATE		DESCRIPTION	POST. REF.	DEBIT	CREDIT	
%							%
&							&
'							'
(							(
)							)
*							*
+							+
,							,
-							-
%.							%.
%%							%%
%&							%&
%'							%'
%(							%(
%)							%)
%*							%*
%+							%+
%,							%,
%-							%-
&.							&.
&%							&%
&&							&&
&'							&'
&(							&(
&)							&)
&*							&*
&+							&+
&,							&,
&-							&-
'.							'.
'%							'%
'&							'&
''							''
'(							'(
')							')
'*							'*

This Page Not Used.

PROBLEM 12-3 ___

A. through G.

<table>
<tr><td colspan="2">JOURNAL</td><td align="right">PAGE</td></tr>
</table>

	DATE	DESCRIPTION	POST. REF.	DEBIT	CREDIT	

PROBLEM 12-3 ___, Concluded

JOURNAL

	DATE		DESCRIPTION	POST. REF.	DEBIT	CREDIT	
%							%
&							&
'							'
(							(
)							)
*							*
+							+
'							'
-							-
%.							%.
%%							%%
%&							%&
%'							%'
%(							%(
%)							%)
%*							%*
%+							%+
%,							%,
%-							%-
&.							&.
&%							&%
&&							&&
&'							&'
&(							&(
&)							&)
&*							&*
&+							&+
&,							&,
&-							&-
'.							'.
'%							'%
'&							'&
"							"
'(							'(
')							')
'*							'*

PROBLEM 12-4 ___

1. and 2.

Common Stock

Paid-In Capital in Excess of Stated Value—Common Stock

Retained Earnings

Treasury Stock

PROBLEM 12-4 ___, Continued

Paid-In Capital from Sale of Treasury Stock

Stock Dividends Distributable

Stock Dividends

Cash Dividends

PROBLEM 12-4 ___, Continued

2.

	DATE		DESCRIPTION	POST. REF.	DEBIT	CREDIT	
%							%
&							&
'							'
(							(
)							)
*							*
+							+
'							'
-							-
%.							%.
%%							%%
%&							%&
%'							%'
%(							%(
%)							%)
%*							%*
%+							%+
%,							%,
%-							%-
&.							&.
&%							&%
&&							&&
&'							&'
&(							&(
&)							&)
&*							&*
&+							&+
&,							&,
&-							&-
'.							'.
'%							'%
'&							'&
''							''
'(							'(
')							')

PROBLEM 12-4 ___, Continued

JOURNAL

	DATE		DESCRIPTION	POST. REF.	DEBIT	CREDIT	
%							%
&							&
'							'
(							(
)							)
*							*
+							+
'							'
-							-
%.							%.
%%							%%
%&							%&
%'							%'
%(							%(
%)							%)
%*							%*
%+							%+
%,							%,
%-							%-
&.							&.
&%							&%
&&							&&
&'							&'
&(							&(
&)							&)
&*							&*
&+							&+
&,							&,
&-							&-
'.							'.
'%							'%
'&							'&
"							"
'(							'(
')							')
'*							'*

PROBLEM 12-4 ___, Concluded

3.

Retained Earnings Statement		

4.

This Page Not Used.

PROBLEM 12-5 ___

JOURNAL

	DATE		DESCRIPTION	POST. REF.	DEBIT	CREDIT	
%							%
&							&
'							'
(							(
)							)
*							*
+							+
'							'
-							-
%.							%.
%%							%%
%&							%&
%'							%'
%(							%(
%)							%)
%*							%*
%+							%+
%,							%,
%-							%-
&.							&.
&%							&%
&&							&&
&'							&'
&(							&(
&)							&)
&*							&*
&+							&+
&,							&,
&-							&-
'.							'.
'%							'%
'&							'&
"							"
'(							'(
')							')
'*							'*

PROBLEM 12-5 ___, Concluded

JOURNAL

	DATE		DESCRIPTION	POST. REF.	DEBIT	CREDIT	
%							%
&							&
'							'
(							(
)							)
*							*
+							+
'							'
-							-
%.							%.
%%							%%
%&							%&
%'							%'
%(							%(
%)							%)
%*							%*
%+							%+
%,							%,
%-							%-
&.							&.
&%							&%
&&							&&
&'							&'
&(							&(
&)							&)
&*							&*
&+							&+
&,							&,
&-							&-
'.							'.
'%							'%
'&							'&
"							"
'(							'(
')							')
'*							'*

COMPREHENSIVE PROBLEM 4

1. A. through J.

JOURNAL

	DATE		DESCRIPTION	POST. REF.	DEBIT	CREDIT	
%							%
&							&
'							'
(							(
)							)
*							*
+							+
'							'
-							-
%.							%.
%%							%%
%&							%&
%'							%'
%(							%(
%)							%)
%*							%*
%+							%+
%,							%,
%-							%-
&.							&.
&%							&%
&&							&&
&'							&'
&(							&(
&)							&)
&*							&*
&+							&+
&,							&,
&-							&-
'.							'.
'%							'%
'&							'&
"							"
'(							'(
')							')

COMPREHENSIVE PROBLEM 4, Continued

JOURNAL

	DATE		DESCRIPTION	POST. REF.	DEBIT	CREDIT	
%							%
&							&
'							'
(							(
)							)
*							*
+							+
'							'
-							-
%.							%.
%%							%%
%&							%&
%'							%'
%(							%(
%)							%)
%*							%*
%+							%+
%,							%,
%-							%-
&.							&.
&%							&%
&&							&&
&'							&'
&(							&(
&)							&)
&*							&*
&+							&+
&,							&,
&-							&-
'.							'.
'%							'%
'&							'&
"							"
'(							'(
')							')
'*							'*

COMPREHENSIVE PROBLEM 4, Continued

2. A.

	Income Statement		

COMPREHENSIVE PROBLEM 4, Continued

Income Statement (continued)

COMPREHENSIVE PROBLEM 4, Continued

B.

Retained Earnings Statement			

COMPREHENSIVE PROBLEM 4, Continued

C.

	Balance Sheet		

COMPREHENSIVE PROBLEM 4, Continued

Balance Sheet (continued)

COMPREHENSIVE PROBLEM 4, Concluded

Balance Sheet (continued)

EXERCISE 13-1

_____
_____
_____
_____
_____
_____
_____
_____
_____
_____
_____
_____
_____
_____

EXERCISE 13-2

A. _____
B. _____
C. _____
D. _____
E. _____
F. _____
G. _____
H. _____

EXERCISE 13-3

A. Net income: _____

B. Paid cash dividends: _____

C. Issued common stock: _____

D. Issued bonds: _____

E. Redeemed bonds: _____

F. Sold long-term investments: _____

G. Purchased treasury stock: _____

H. Sold equipment: _____

I. Issued preferred stock: _____

J. Purchased buildings: _____

K. Purchased patents: _____

EXERCISE 13-4

A. Decrease in inventory: _____

B. Increase in accounts receivable: _____

C. Increase in accounts payable: _____

D. Loss on retirement of long-term debt: _____

E. Depreciation of fixed assets: _____

F. Decrease in notes receivable due in 60 days from customers: _____

G. Increase in salaries payable: _____

H. Decrease in prepaid expenses: _____

I. Amortization of patent: _____

J. Increase in notes payable due in 120 days to vendors: _____

K. Gain on disposal of fixed assets: _____

EXERCISE 13-5

A.

EXERCISE 13-5, Concluded

B. _____
_____
_____
_____
_____
_____
_____
_____
_____
_____
_____
_____
_____
_____
_____
_____

EXERCISE 13-6

A.

EXERCISE 13-6, Concluded

B. _____

_____

_____

_____

EXERCISE 13-7

A.

EXERCISE 13-7, Concluded

B. _____

_____

_____

_____

_____

_____

_____

_____

_____

_____

_____

_____

_____

EXERCISE 13-8

EXERCISE 13-9

EXERCISE 13-10

EXERCISE 13-11

EXERCISE 13-12

EXERCISE 13-13

EXERCISE 13-14

_____
_____
_____
_____
_____
_____

EXERCISE 13-15

A.

EXERCISE 13-15, Concluded

B. _____

_____

_____

_____

_____

_____

_____

_____

_____

_____

_____

_____

_____

_____

_____

_____

_____

_____

_____

_____

_____

_____

EXERCISE 13-16

A.

Cash Flows from Operating Activities		

B. _____

_____

_____

_____

_____

_____

_____

_____

EXERCISE 13-17

A.

Statement of Cash Flows		

EXERCISE 13-17, Concluded

B. _____

_____

_____

_____

_____

_____

_____

_____

_____

_____

_____

_____

_____

_____

_____

_____

_____

_____

_____

_____

_____

EXERCISE 13-18

_____

_____

_____

_____

_____

_____

_____

_____

_____

_____

_____

_____

_____

_____

_____

_____

_____

_____

_____

_____

_____

_____

_____

_____

EXERCISE 13-18, Continued

(Optional)

	Statement of Cash Flows		

EXERCISE 13-18, Concluded

Statement of Cash Flows (continued)

APPENDIX 2 EXERCISE 13-19

A.

B.

C.

APPENDIX 2 EXERCISE 13-20

A.

B.

APPENDIX 2 EXERCISE 13-21

A.

Computations:

APPENDIX 2 EXERCISE 13-21, Concluded

B. _____

_____

_____

_____

_____

_____

_____

_____

_____

_____

_____

_____

_____

APPENDIX 2 EXERCISE 13-22

Computations:

PROBLEM 13-1 ___

Statement of Cash Flows		

PROBLEM 13-1 ___, Continued

Statement of Cash Flows (continued)

PROBLEM 13-1 ___, Continued

The use of this form is not required unless so indicated by the instructor.

	A	B	C	D	E
1					
2		Spreadsheet (Work Sheet) for Statement of Cash Flows			
3					
4		Balance, _____	Transactions		Balance, _____
5	Account Title		Debit	Credit	
6					
7					
8					
9					
10					
11					
12					
13					
14					
15					
16					
17					
18					
19					
20					
21					
22					
23					
24					
25					
26					
27					
28					
29					
30					
31					
32					
33					
34					
35					
36					
37					
38					
39					
40					
41					
42					
43					
44					
45					

PROBLEM 13-1 ___, Concluded

	A	B	C	D	E
1					
2	Spreadsheet (Work Sheet) for Statement of Cash Flows (continued)				
3					
4	Account Title	Balance, _____	Transactions		Balance, _____
5			Debit	Credit	
6					
7					
8					
9					
10					
11					
12					
13					
14					
15					
16					
17					
18					
19					
20					
21					
22					
23					
24					
25					
26					
27					
28					
29					
30					
31					
32					
33					
34					
35					
36					
37					
38					
39					
40					
41					
42					
43					
44					
45					

PROBLEM 13-2 ___

Statement of Cash Flows			

PROBLEM 13-2 ___, Continued

Statement of Cash Flows (continued)

PROBLEM 13-2 ___, Continued

The use of this form is not required unless so indicated by the instructor.

	A	B	C	D	E
1					
2		Spreadsheet (Work Sheet) for Statement of Cash Flows			
3					
4		Balance, _____	Transactions		Balance, _____
5	Account Title		Debit	Credit	
6					
7					
8					
9					
10					
11					
12					
13					
14					
15					
16					
17					
18					
19					
20					
21					
22					
23					
24					
25					
26					
27					
28					
29					
30					
31					
32					
33					
34					
35					
36					
37					
38					
39					
40					
41					
42					
43					
44					
45					

PROBLEM 13-2 ____, Concluded

	A	B	C	D	E
1					
2		Spreadsheet (Work Sheet) for Statement of Cash Flows (continued)			
3					
4	Account Title	Balance, _____	Transactions		Balance, _____
5			Debit	Credit	
6					
7					
8					
9					
10					
11					
12					
13					
14					
15					
16					
17					
18					
19					
20					
21					
22					
23					
24					
25					
26					
27					
28					
29					
30					
31					
32					
33					
34					
35					
36					
37					
38					
39					
40					
41					
42					
43					
44					
45					

PROBLEM 13-3 ___

Statement of Cash Flows		

PROBLEM 13-3 ___, Continued

Statement of Cash Flows (continued)		

PROBLEM 13-3 ___, Continued

The use of this form is not required unless so indicated by the instructor.

	A	B	C	D	E
1					
2	Spreadsheet (Work Sheet) for Statement of Cash Flows				
3					
4		Balance, _____	Transactions		Balance, _____
5	Account Title		Debit	Credit	
6					
7					
8					
9					
10					
11					
12					
13					
14					
15					
16					
17					
18					
19					
20					
21					
22					
23					
24					
25					
26					
27					
28					
29					
30					
31					
32					
33					
34					
35					
36					
37					
38					
39					
40					
41					
42					
43					
44					
45					

PROBLEM 13-3 ___, Concluded

	A	B	C	D	E
1					
2		Spreadsheet (Work Sheet) for Statement of Cash Flows (continued)			
3					
4		Balance, _____	Transactions		Balance, _____
5	Account Title		Debit	Credit	
6					
7					
8					
9					
10					
11					
12					
13					
14					
15					
16					
17					
18					
19					
20					
21					
22					
23					
24					
25					
26					
27					
28					
29					
30					
31					
32					
33					
34					
35					
36					
37					
38					
39					
40					
41					
42					
43					
44					
45					

APPENDIX 2 PROBLEM 13-4 ___

Statement of Cash Flows		

APPENDIX 2 PROBLEM 13-4 ___, Concluded

Computations:

APPENDIX 2 PROBLEM 13-5 ___

Statement of Cash Flows		

APPENDIX 2 PROBLEM 13-5 ___, Concluded

Computations:

EXERCISE 14-1

A.

	Comparative Income Statement			

	CURRENT YEAR		PREVIOUS YEAR	
	AMOUNT	PERCENT	AMOUNT	PERCENT

B. _____

_____

_____

_____

_____

_____

_____

_____

EXERCISE 14-2

A.

Comparative Income Statement (in thousands of dollars)

	CURRENT YEAR		PREVIOUS YEAR	
	AMOUNT	PERCENT	AMOUNT	PERCENT

EXERCISE 14-2, Concluded

B. _____

_____
_____
_____
_____
_____
_____
_____
_____
_____
_____
_____
_____
_____
_____
_____
_____
_____
_____
_____
_____

EXERCISE 14-3

A.

| | TANNENHILL COMPANY | | ELECTRONICS INDUSTRY AVERAGE |
	AMOUNT	PERCENT	

Common-Sized Income Statement

B. _____

_____

_____

_____

_____

_____

_____

_____

_____

_____

_____

_____

_____

_____

_____

_____

EXERCISE 14-4

Comparative Balance Sheet

	CURRENT YEAR		PREVIOUS YEAR	
	AMOUNT	PERCENT	AMOUNT	PERCENT

EXERCISE 14-5

A.

Comparative Income Statement

	CURRENT YEAR AMOUNT	PREVIOUS YEAR AMOUNT	INCREASE (DECREASE)	
			AMOUNT	PERCENT

EXERCISE 14-5, Concluded

B. _____

_____

_____

_____

_____

_____

_____

_____

EXERCISE 14-6

A. (1) Working Capital = _____

_____

Current Year: _____

_____

Previous Year: _____

_____

(2) Current Ratio = _____

_____

Current Year: _____

_____

Previous Year: _____

_____

(3) Quick Ratio = _____

_____

Current Year: _____

_____

Previous Year: _____

_____

B. _____

_____

_____

_____

_____

_____

EXERCISE 14-7

A. (1) Current Ratio = _____

_____

Current Year: _____

_____

Previous Year: _____

_____

(2) Quick Ratio = _____

_____

Current Year: _____

_____

Previous Year: _____

_____

B. _____

_____

_____

_____

_____

_____

_____

_____

EXERCISE 14-8

A. _____

_____

_____

_____

_____

_____

_____

_____

_____

_____

_____

_____

_____

_____

_____

_____

_____

_____

_____

_____

_____

_____

_____

_____

_____

_____

_____

_____

B. _____

_____

_____

_____

_____

EXERCISE 14-9

A. **(1)** Accounts Receivable Turnover = _____

_____

20Y3: _____

20Y2: _____

(2) Number of Days' Sales in Receivables = _____

_____

20Y3: _____

20Y2: _____

B. _____

_____

_____

_____

_____

_____

_____

_____

_____

_____

_____

EXERCISE 14-10

A. **(1)** Accounts Receivable Turnover = _____

_____

Xavier: _____

Lestrade: _____

(2) Number of Days' Sales in Receivables = _____

_____

Xavier: _____

Lestrade: _____

_____

EXERCISE 14-10, Concluded

B. _____

_____

_____

_____

_____

_____

_____

_____

_____

_____

EXERCISE 14-11

A. (1) Inventory Turnover = _____

_____

Current Year: _____

_____

Previous Year: _____

_____

(2) Number of Days' Sales in Inventory = _____

_____

Current Year: _____

_____

Previous Year: _____

_____

B. _____

_____

_____

_____

_____

_____

_____

_____

EXERCISE 14-12

A. (1) Inventory Turnover = _____

_____

QT: _____

_____

Elppa: _____

_____

(2) Number of Days' Sales in Inventory = _____

_____

QT: _____

_____

Elppa: _____

_____

B. _____

_____

_____

_____

_____

_____

_____

_____

_____

_____

_____

_____

_____

_____

_____

_____

_____

_____

_____

_____

EXERCISE 14-13

A. Ratio of Liabilities to Stockholders' Equity = _____

_____

Current Year: _____

_____

Previous Year: _____

_____

B. Times Interest Earned = _____

_____

Current Year: _____

_____

Previous Year: _____

_____

C. _____

_____

_____

_____

_____

_____

_____

_____

_____

EXERCISE 14-14

A. Ratio of Liabilities to Stockholders' Equity = _____

_____

Hasbro: _____

_____

Mattel, Inc.: _____

_____

B. Times Interest Earned = _____

_____

Hasbro: _____

_____

Mattel, Inc.: _____

_____

EXERCISE 14-14, Concluded

C. _____

_____

_____

_____

_____

_____

_____

_____

_____

_____

_____

_____

_____

_____

EXERCISE 14-15

A. Ratio of Liabilities to Stockholders' Equity = _____

_____

Mondelez: _____

_____

Hershey: _____

_____

B. Ratio of Fixed Assets to Long-Term Liabilities = _____

_____

Mondelez: _____

_____

Hershey: _____

_____

EXERCISE 14-15, Concluded

C. _____

_____

_____

_____

_____

_____

_____

_____

_____

_____

_____

_____

_____

_____

_____

_____

_____

_____

_____

_____

EXERCISE 14-16

A. Asset Turnover = _____

_____

YRC: _____

_____

Union Pacific: _____

_____

C.H. Robinson: _____

_____

EXERCISE 14-16, Concluded

B. _____

_____

_____

_____

_____

_____

_____

_____

_____

_____

_____

_____

_____

_____

_____

_____

_____

_____

_____

_____

_____

_____

_____

_____

_____

_____

_____

_____

EXERCISE 14-17

A. Return on Total Assets = _____

_____

20Y7: _____

_____

20Y6: _____

_____

Return on Stockholders' Equity = _____

_____

20Y7: _____

_____

20Y6: _____

_____

Return on Common Stockholders' Equity = _____

_____

20Y7: _____

_____

20Y6: _____

_____

B. _____

_____

_____

_____

_____

_____

_____

_____

_____

_____

_____

_____

_____

EXERCISE 14-18

A. Return on Total Assets = _____

_____

Fiscal Year 3: _____

_____

Fiscal Year 2: _____

_____

B. Return on Stockholders' Equity = _____

_____

Fiscal Year 3: _____

_____

Fiscal Year 2: _____

_____

C. _____

_____

_____

_____

_____

_____

_____

_____

_____

_____

D. _____

_____

_____

_____

_____

_____

_____

_____

_____

_____

_____

EXERCISE 14-19

A. Ratio of Fixed Assets to Long-Term Liabilities = _____

_____

_____

_____

_____

B. Ratio of Liabilities to Stockholders' Equity = _____

_____

_____

_____

_____

C. Asset Turnover = _____

_____

_____

_____

_____

D. Return on Total Assets = _____

_____

_____

_____

_____

E. Return on Stockholders' Equity = _____

_____

_____

_____

_____

F. Return on Common Stockholders' Equity = _____

_____

_____

_____

_____

EXERCISE 14-20

A. Times Interest Earned = _____

_____

_____

_____

_____

B. Earnings per Share on Common Stock = _____

_____

_____

_____

_____

C. Price-Earnings Ratio = _____

_____

_____

_____

_____

D. Dividends per Share of Common Stock = _____

_____

_____

_____

_____

E. Dividend Yield = _____

_____

_____

_____

_____

EXERCISE 14-21

A. Earnings per Share = _____

_____

_____

_____

_____

B. Price-Earnings Ratio = _____

_____

_____

_____

_____

C. Dividends per Share = _____

_____

_____

_____

_____

D. Dividend Yield = _____

_____

_____

_____

_____

EXERCISE 14-22

A. Price-Earnings Ratio = _____

_____

Deere & Company: _____

_____

Google: _____

_____

The Coca-Cola Company: _____

_____

Dividend Yield = _____

_____

Deere & Company: _____

_____

Google: _____

_____

The Coca-Cola Company: _____

_____

B. _____

_____

_____

_____

_____

_____

_____

_____

_____

_____

_____

_____

_____

_____

_____

_____

_____

_____

_____

_____

APPENDIX 1 EXERCISE 14-23

A. Earnings per share on income before discontinued operations:

Earnings Before Discontinued Operations per Share on Common Stock = _____

B. Earnings per Share on Common Stock = _____

APPENDIX 1 EXERCISE 14-24

A.

Partial Income Statement

APPENDIX 1 EXERCISE 14-24, Concluded

B.

	Partial Income Statement		

APPENDIX 1 EXERCISE 14-25

A. _____

_____

_____

_____

_____

_____

B. _____

_____

_____

_____

_____

_____

_____

APPENDIX 2 EXERCISE 14-26

A.

Income Statement

B.

Income Statement

Statement of Comprehensive Income

PROBLEM 14-1 ___

1.

Comparative Income Statement

	20Y2	20Y1	INCREASE (DECREASE)	
			AMOUNT	PERCENT

2. _____

_____

_____

_____

_____

_____

_____

_____

_____

_____

This Page Not Used.

PROBLEM 14-2 ____

1.

	20Y2		20Y1	
	AMOUNT	PERCENT	AMOUNT	PERCENT

Comparative Income Statement

2. _____

_____

_____

_____

_____

_____

_____

_____

_____

_____

_____

_____

This Page Not Used.

PROBLEM 14-3 ___

1. A. Working Capital = _____

_____

_____

_____

_____

B. Current Ratio = _____

_____

_____

_____

_____

C. Quick Ratio = _____

_____

_____

_____

_____

PROBLEM 14-3 ____, Concluded

2.

Transaction	Working Capital	Current Ratio	Quick Ratio
A.			
B.			
C.			
D.			
E.			
F.			
G.			
H.			
I.			
J.			

Supporting calculations:

Transaction	Current Assets	Quick Assets	Current Liabilities
A.			
B.			
C.			
D.			
E.			
F.			
G.			
H.			
I.			
J.			

PROBLEM 14-4 ___

1. through 18.

1. Working Capital: _____

Ratio	Numerator	Denominator	Calculated Value
2. Current ratio			
3. Quick ratio			
4. Accounts receivable turnover			
5. Number of days' sales in receivables			
6. Inventory turnover			
7. Number of days' sales in inventory			
8. Ratio of fixed assets to long-term liabilities			
9. Ratio of liabilities to stockholders' equity			
10. Times interest earned			
11. Asset turnover			
12. Return on total assets			
13. Return on stockholders' equity			
14. Return on common stockholders' equity			
15. Earnings per share on common stock			
16. Price-earnings ratio			
17. Dividends per share of common stock			
18. Dividend yield			

This Page Not Used.

PROBLEM 14-5 ___

1. A.

*(y-axis label: **Return on Total Assets**; x-axis label: **Year**)*

Return on Total Assets = _____

_____

20Y8: _____	20Y5: _____
_____	_____
20Y7: _____	20Y4: _____
_____	_____
20Y6: _____	
_____	

PROBLEM 14-5 ___ , Continued

B.

Return on Stockholders' Equity

Year

Return on Stockholders' Equity = _____

_____

20Y8: _____   20Y5: _____

_____

20Y7: _____   20Y4: _____

_____

20Y6: _____

_____

PROBLEM 14-5 ____, Continued

C.

Times Interest Earned

Year

Times Interest Earned = _____

_____

20Y8: _____   20Y5: _____

_____   _____

20Y7: _____   20Y4: _____

_____   _____

20Y6: _____

_____

PROBLEM 14-5 ___, Continued

D.

Ratio of Liabilities to Stockholders' Equity

Year

Ratio of Liabilities to Stockholders' Equity = _____

_____

20Y8: _____   20Y5: _____

_____

20Y7: _____   20Y4: _____

_____

20Y6: _____

_____

PROBLEM 14-5 ___ , Concluded

2. _____

_____

_____

_____

_____

_____

_____

_____

_____

_____

_____

_____

_____

_____

_____

_____

_____

_____

_____

_____

_____

_____

This Page Not Used.

NIKE, INC., PROBLEM

1. A. through M.

	FISCAL 2015	FISCAL 2014

NIKE, INC., PROBLEM, Continued

	FISCAL 2015	FISCAL 2014

NIKE, INC., PROBLEM, Continued

	FISCAL 2015	FISCAL 2014

NIKE, INC., PROBLEM, Continued

2. A. through M.

_____

_____

_____

_____

_____

_____

_____

_____

_____

_____

_____

_____

_____

_____

_____

_____

_____

_____

_____

_____

_____

_____

_____

_____

_____

_____

_____

_____

_____

_____

_____

_____

_____

_____

_____

NIKE, INC., PROBLEM, Concluded

This Page Not Used.

EXERCISE D-1

A., B., and C.

JOURNAL   PAGE

	DATE		DESCRIPTION	POST. REF.	DEBIT	CREDIT	
1							1
2							2
3							3
4							4
5							5
6							6
7							7
8							8
9							9
10							10
11							11
12							12
13							13
14							14
15							15
16							16
17							17
18							18
19							19
20							20

Computations:

EXERCISE D-2

A., B., C., and D.

JOURNAL

PAGE

	DATE		DESCRIPTION	POST. REF.	DEBIT	CREDIT	
1							1
2							2
3							3
4							4
5							5
6							6
7							7
8							8
9							9
10							10
11							11
12							12
13							13
14							14
15							15
16							16
17							17
18							18
19							19
20							20
21							21
22							22
23							23
24							24
25							25
26							26
27							27
28							28

EXERCISE D-3

A., B., C., and D.

JOURNAL   PAGE

	DATE		DESCRIPTION	POST. REF.	DEBIT	CREDIT	
1							1
2							2
3							3
4							4
5							5
6							6
7							7
8							8
9							9
10							10
11							11
12							12
13							13
14							14
15							15
16							16
17							17
18							18
19							19
20							20
21							21
22							22
23							23
24							24
25							25
26							26
27							27
28							28

EXERCISE D-4

JOURNAL

	DATE		DESCRIPTION	POST. REF.	DEBIT	CREDIT	
1							1
2							2
3							3
4							4
5							5
6							6
7							7
8							8
9							9
10							10
11							11
12							12
13							13
14							14
15							15
16							16
17							17
18							18
19							19
20							20
21							21
22							22
23							23
24							24

EXERCISE D-5

JOURNAL   PAGE

	DATE		DESCRIPTION	POST. REF.	DEBIT	CREDIT	
1							1
2							2
3							3
4							4
5							5
6							6
7							7
8							8
9							9
10							10
11							11
12							12
13							13
14							14
15							15
16							16
17							17
18							18
19							19
20							20
21							21
22							22
23							23
24							24
25							25
26							26
27							27
28							28
29							29
30							30
31							31
32							32
33							33
34							34
35							35
36							36

EXERCISE D-6

JOURNAL

	DATE		DESCRIPTION	POST. REF.	DEBIT	CREDIT	
1							1
2							2
3							3
4							4
5							5
6							6
7							7
8							8
9							9
10							10
11							11
12							12
13							13
14							14
15							15
16							16
17							17
18							18
19							19
20							20

EXERCISE D-7

A.

		JOURNAL				PAGE

	DATE	DESCRIPTION	POST. REF.	DEBIT	CREDIT	
1						1
2						2
3						3
4						4
5						5
6						6
7						7
8						8
9						9
10						10
11						11
12						12
13						13
14						14
15						15
16						16
17						17
18						18
19						19
20						20
21						21
22						22
23						23
24						24

B.

EXERCISE D-8

		JOURNAL			PAGE
DATE		DESCRIPTION	POST. REF.	DEBIT	CREDIT
1					
2					
3					
4					
5					
6					
7					
8					

Computations:

EXERCISE D-9

A.

	DATE		DESCRIPTION	POST. REF.	DEBIT	CREDIT	
1							1
2							2
3							3
4							4
5							5
6							6
7							7
8							8
9							9
10							10
11							11
12							12
13							13
14							14
15							15
16							16
17							17
18							18

JOURNAL   PAGE

B. _____

_____

_____

_____

_____

_____

_____

_____

EXERCISE D-10

JOURNAL   PAGE _____

	DATE		DESCRIPTION	POST. REF.	DEBIT	CREDIT	
1							1
2							2
3							3
4							4
5							5
6							6
7							7
8							8

EXERCISE D-11

JOURNAL   PAGE _____

	DATE		DESCRIPTION	POST. REF.	DEBIT	CREDIT	
1							1
2							2
3							3
4							4
5							5
6							6
7							7
8							8

Computations:

EXERCISE D-12

A.

JOURNAL   PAGE

	DATE		DESCRIPTION	POST. REF.	DEBIT	CREDIT	
1							1
2							2
3							3
4							4
5							5
6							6
7							7
8							8
9							9
10							10
11							11
12							12
13							13
14							14
15							15

B. _____

_____

_____

_____

_____

_____

_____

_____

EXERCISE D-13

A.

JOURNAL   PAGE

	DATE		DESCRIPTION	POST. REF.	DEBIT	CREDIT	
1							1
2							2
3							3
4							4
5							5
6							6
7							7

Computations:

B. _____

_____

_____

_____

_____

_____

_____

_____

_____

EXERCISE D-14

A.

Balance Sheet (selected items)

Computations:

B.

Balance Sheet (selected items)

EXTRA FORMS
JOURNAL

PAGE

	DATE		DESCRIPTION	POST. REF.	DEBIT	CREDIT	
1							1
2							2
3							3
4							4
5							5
6							6
7							7
8							8
9							9
10							10
11							11
12							12
13							13
14							14
15							15
16							16
17							17
18							18
19							19
20							20
21							21
22							22
23							23
24							24
25							25
26							26
27							27
28							28
29							29
30							30
31							31
32							32
33							33
34							34
35							35
36							36

EXTRA FORMS
JOURNAL

PAGE

	DATE		DESCRIPTION	POST. REF.	DEBIT	CREDIT	
1							1
2							2
3							3
4							4
5							5
6							6
7							7
8							8
9							9
10							10
11							11
12							12
13							13
14							14
15							15
16							16
17							17
18							18
19							19
20							20
21							21
22							22
23							23
24							24
25							25
26							26
27							27
28							28
29							29
30							30
31							31
32							32
33							33
34							34
35							35
36							36

EXTRA FORMS
JOURNAL

	DATE		DESCRIPTION	POST. REF.	DEBIT	CREDIT	
1							1
2							2
3							3
4							4
5							5
6							6
7							7
8							8
9							9
10							10
11							11
12							12
13							13
14							14
15							15
16							16
17							17
18							18
19							19
20							20
21							21
22							22
23							23
24							24
25							25
26							26
27							27
28							28
29							29
30							30
31							31
32							32
33							33
34							34
35							35
36							36

EXTRA FORMS

EXTRA FORMS

EXTRA FORMS

EXTRA FORMS

EXTRA FORMS

EXTRA FORMS

CPSIA information can be obtained
at www.ICGtesting.com
Printed in the USA
FFHW010809031118
49252726-53479FF